All You Have to Do Is Listen

Music from the Inside Out

ROB KAPILOW

LINCOLN CENTER | for the Performing Arts

WILEY

John Wiley & Sons, Inc.

Published by John Wiley & Sons, Inc., Hoboken, New Jersey
Published simultaneously in Canada

For general information about our other products and services, please contact our Customer Care Department within the United States at (800) 762-2974, outside the United States at (317) 572-3993 or fax (317) 572-4002.

Wiley also publishes its books in a variety of electronic formats. Some content that appears in print may not be available in electronic books. For more information about Wiley products, visit our web site at www.wiley.com.

ISBN 978-0-470-38544-9

Printed in the United States of America

10 9 8 7 6 5 4 3 2 1

To the memory of Nadia Boulanger—the greatest teacher
of music and listening I have ever known—
and to my wife, Claire, and my three children, Benjamin,
Sarah, and Adam: they are the music of my life.

CONTENTS

PREFACE

Though I have spent more than twenty years trying to help listeners hear more in great music, for the first seventeen of those years, I never even considered writing a book. To write about music in any kind of meaningful detail requires that the reader be able to hear the music you are describing, and until recently this has been an obstacle faced by all books and printed materials written for the general public. Though a trained musician might be capable of looking at musical notation in a book and hearing the sound in his head, for most untrained people this is simply not possible. Consequently, in the past, a book about music either had to be so general as to be understandable without reference to the actual sounds of a piece, or if the book included detailed examples in musical notation, it largely excluded the general public without the specialized knowledge required to hear or play the examples. About ten years ago, some books began to include CDs to try to help solve the problem, but their relationship to individual examples or detailed descriptions was cumbersome and complicated and ultimately did little to solve the general listener's problem.

Recent advances in technology, however, have improved the situation, and these advances are what made me eager to write this book in the first place. When I do a live program with musicians present, I am able to take a small amount of music and work with it measure by measure—take it apart instrument by instrument, change it, highlight key details of rhythm, melody, and harmony, and then put the excerpt back together again. Now, thanks to new Web-based technology, I can do something similar in book form for all listeners—whether they can read music or not. There are ninety-three musical examples in this volume that are printed in musical notation in the book itself but are also printed on the Web site associated with this book. (See "How to Use the Web Site.") All the excerpts in musical notation can be heard on the book's Web site and they are designed to scroll in real time with a visual scrollbar as the music is playing. In addition, key points from the book's discussion of each example are written on the musical notation on the Web site. So if the text refers to an interesting chord in measure 4, as the music plays and scrolls to measure 4, the chord will be marked in such a way that any listener can hear and see the reference whether or not he can read music. Though an experienced musician might be able to hear all of the examples simply by reading the printed notation, the Web site opens up the book's musical content and discussion to any listener regardless of his musical background or training. A first-time listener might require more than one hearing of each example to fully grasp its content, but I guarantee that the repetition will be valuable.

It is my deepest hope that this new technology will allow all interested music lovers, with or without musical training, to have access to a kind of detailed musical discussion that was previously available in book form only to those with prior musical training. Though the examples might require effort and attention to master, in the end, all you have to do is listen.

ACKNOWLEDGMENTS

To write a book requires the foolhardy belief that with all that has already been written, you might still have something of value to say. Since the thought would never have occurred to me on my own, I would like to thank several key people who over my strenuous objections talked me into considering the possibility that I might be able to write something that could help listeners deepen their appreciation of music. First of all, two people at Lincoln Center—its president, Reynold Levy, and Vice President of Programming, Jane Moss—who for no apparent reason believed in this book without having the slightest idea what form it would ultimately take. At John Wiley & Sons, my editor, guiding spirit, partner, and perfect reader, Hana Lane, who was the kind of supportive yet critical taskmaster every first-time author should be lucky enough to have. My literary agent, Carl Brandt, who through three years of doubt and confusion as the project took shape was not only a willing ear for every new idea and suggestion I had, but also an unfailingly enthusiastic believer, critic, and facilitator. Louise Barder and the staff at 21C Media who were advisors, supporters, and sounding boards on every aspect of the project. My agent at IMG, Charles LeTourneau, who embodies the spirit of "yes," wholeheartedly championed the project, jumping in eagerly to help make it possible even though by no stretch of the imagination should it have fallen under his purview.

I cannot give enough credit to my two superb assistants at Juilliard,

Nicholas Csicsko and Alexander Popov, who spent countless hours mastering the technology at the heart of this book in order to make the musical examples spring so beautifully to life. Without their dedication, perseverance, and painstaking work, this book in its current form would not have been possible.

Perhaps most of all, however, I would like to thank the many listeners who responded to my programs either on National Public Radio, CD, or live in concert. Ultimately, it was watching and hearing their enthusiasm as they "got" a phrase of music, or connected with a piece for the first time, that inspired me to write this book in the first place. They convinced me that a deeper appreciation of music was not only meaningful and valuable but also utterly obtainable. They convinced me that all you have to do is listen.

HOW TO USE THE WEB SITE

To complement the text of this book, we have created a Web site where you can see and listen to the musical examples. Watch the scrollbar move along with the notes as they're played, or download the .mp4 files to your computer.

To listen to or download the files, follow these steps:

1. Enter www.wiley.com/go/allyouhavetodoislisten into your Internet browser.

2. Click on the chapter you're looking for in the list located on the left side of the page OR click on the link labeled "Download All Examples" to save all the examples to a location of your choice on your computer.

3. Click on the numbered example you want to listen to.

If you want to upload the files to an .mp4-compatible portable device, such as an iPod, follow your portable device's directions on uploading an .mp4 file.

That's all there is to it. Have fun and remember, all you have to do is listen.

[PRELUDE]

All You Have to Do
Is Listen

Though I did not realize it at the time, the idea for this book began more than twenty years ago on the 11:20 p.m. Metro-North train from New York City to New Haven, Connecticut. Just after finishing graduate school, I was fortunate to get my first job as an assistant professor of music at Yale and the conductor of the Yale Symphony Orchestra. Toward the end of my six-year stint at Yale, I had the opportunity to conduct the Tony Award–winning musical *Nine* on Broadway, and for a brief period I foolishly tried to do both jobs at the same time. I would teach and conduct in New Haven during the day, race to the train, conduct the evening show on Broadway, and take the 11:20 train home after the show. The daily train ride from New York to New Haven gave me time to think about the enormous differences between the musical worlds of Broadway and Yale, and forced me to recognize some uncomfortable yet unavoidable truths.

Anyone who has ever spoken to an audience, even an audience of one, knows what it feels like when his message is getting across, when the listener is "getting it." On Broadway, not only were large numbers of people eager to pay considerable sums of money night after night to see the show, but they also "got it." The show clearly spoke a musical language that America understood. Unfortunately, I could not say the same thing about the symphony concerts I conducted or attended. Though there were certainly some individuals who were as fluent in the language of classical music as they were in the music of Broadway, by and large audiences in America simply did not "get" classical music the way they got *Nine*. Yet I was absolutely certain that they *could* get it, and that I could help.

I began trying to create programs to help people hear more in all kinds of music: from Gregorian chant to Bach concertos, from Mozart sonatas to Haydn string quartets, from Beethoven symphonies to Steve Reich chamber music, Duke Ellington big-band suites, and Stephen Sondheim theater songs. The *What Makes It Great?* series I started eighteen years ago on National Public Radio (NPR) focused on a tiny amount of music each week—often no more than twenty or thirty seconds per program. In a kind of musical exercise equivalent to the close reading of poetry, I would look at each excerpt measure by measure to see what made it tick and what made it great. One of the things I discovered in program after program was that the difference between good and great is both enormous and infinitesimal. It is hundreds of small, inspired choices made by a composer, note by note, chord by chord, and rhythm by rhythm. I would frequently recompose passages by changing a single rhythm, or a note in a melody or a chord, and suddenly a catchy rhythm, a soaring melody, or a poignant harmony would become dull and lifeless. Over time, I also discovered that it was not only possible to get people to hear all of these fantastic details that race by at lightning speed in great music, but that it was possible to do so with practically no technical vocabulary. It wasn't so much that music needed to be "explained," it was that it needed truly to be heard. Once people were encouraged in a focused way to "listen to this chord," "pay attention to this rhythm," or "notice this variation," they "got it," in as visceral a way as they "got" the music of *Nine*.

As I expanded these short NPR programs to full-length evenings in concert halls around the country, I began to realize that if there are a thousand people at a concert, there are a thousand different performances occurring simultaneously. What is being played is not the same as what is being heard. Ralph Waldo Emerson wrote, "It is the good reader that makes the good book": a quotation that goes to the heart of this book. Without great listeners, great music is the proverbial tree falling in the forest with no one around to hear it. But how does someone become a better listener?

Let me state a personal prejudice at the outset. Though there is a vast amount of fascinating and valuable biographical and historical information available about music, I believe the core of great listening has less to do with facts and far more to do with our ability to pay attention, listen closely, and notice. This book is about learning to listen to music from the inside out: from the composer's point of view. It's about all of the things in a piece of music that composers want you to hear but are so often missed: not only the moment-by-moment sensual sound of music, but the way its story is told in notes—what I will call the plot. In this book, I have tried to introduce topics as they would naturally arise in listening to a composition from beginning to end, so that the focus gradually widens as the book progresses: from idea, to phrase, to section, to movement, to form. As in a piece of music, many of the key themes and ideas that are introduced in the opening chapters only acquire their full significance as they return throughout the book in ever wider contexts.

Unlike my *What Makes It Great?* programs, which focus on getting inside a single piece of music, the goal of this book is broader: namely, to get at the larger listening principles that lie behind these individual programs. I want to give you a set of listening tools that will enrich your musical experiences whether you are a newcomer to classical music or a veteran concertgoer. Each chapter is designed to serve as a point of entry to some key aspect of musical style that once it is understood can be heard in a wide variety of repertoire. Many of the concepts, analogies, and metaphors in this book are drawn from everyday experience. Some of these ideas might seem almost self-evident on first reading, but the more you work with them and apply them to the music you know, the more you will begin to hear. There is one point I want to be clear about: though I will attempt throughout this book to help you recognize what composers want you to hear, it is only important that you notice these things, not that you be able to articulate them in any way. When studying anything—whether a foreign language, cooking, or golf—the learning of fundamentals is highly conscious at first (subject-object-verb-tense, sear-fold-baste, left arm stiff-right arm bent-turn hips, etc.) but ultimately becomes a reflex. My hope is that you will gradually internalize the book's approach, and it will simply become part of how you listen.

One of the challenges of listening to a piece of music is the fact that music happens in real time. If you are reading a poem or a novel you can read at whatever speed you like and go back and reread at your leisure. Similarly, if you are looking at a painting in a museum you can stop and study it, stepping back or moving closer, for as long as you wish. How much time you spend is up to you. But a piece of music has time embedded in it. No matter how attentively or casually you listen, it takes a fixed number of minutes for a piece of music to play, and the experience moves at a pace determined not by the listener but by the composer (and performer). If you have a recording, you can repeat the experience as many times as you wish, but unless you can play from the score yourself, each listening experience takes a fixed amount of time. Listening to a piece of music happens in real time, from beginning to end, without stopping. It is a straight-through experience. Like playing a sport.

An athlete practices and trains in order to be able to operate at maximum efficiency in competition when there is minimal time for rational thought. A tennis player, for example, will analyze every aspect of his serve in a highly deliberate way, taking the motion apart element by element. The toss first. Then the racquet arm. Then the feet. Only after all of the elements have been carefully analyzed in isolation are they put back together again. This conscious practice is designed to make these movements and gestures unconscious so that they will simply happen spontaneously when the player serves in a match.

Likewise, the purpose of this book is to study the listening process—to "train"—so that the knowledge and principles gained will be available to you as a piece of music is played—to make what is at first highly conscious a reflex. What composers want from listeners isn't after-the-fact, rational understanding, but the capacity to follow, grasp, and be moved by a piece of music as it is happening. In *How Does a Poem Mean?* John Ciardi wrote, "The only reason for taking a poem apart is that it may then be put together again more richly." Similarly, the sole point of taking music apart is in order to put it back together more meaningfully. Though this book makes no pretense of being comprehensive or presenting a universal system or theory of any kind, it is my deepest belief that if you listen carefully to the musical examples in this book until you really hear them and internalize their principles, it will change the way you hear music.

It will help you hear a piece of music in real time and truly follow its thread as the notes go by. Musical knowledge is real when it becomes simply how you listen. From beginning to end. To Mozart or the Gershwins. Once you have trained your ear, all you will have to do is listen.

[1]

Does Music Have a Plot?

The real voyage of discovery consists not in seeking new landscapes but in having new eyes.

—MARCEL PROUST

Several years ago, in an effort to widen the audience for a *What Makes It Great?* program in Lincoln, Nebraska, I went on an AM talk-radio show called *Coffee Talk*. I offered four free tickets to the caller who hated classical music the most and asked people to call in and tell me why they hated it, or even why they hated people who liked it. The clear winner was Anne, who said she hated classical music because "it's long, boring, and *has no plot*" (italics added). Was she right? Or does music have a plot? If so, what is it? Why is it important? How can we begin to hear it?

To begin, I want to make a basic distinction between what Aaron Copland calls listening to music on "the sensuous plane"—"for the sheer pleasure of the musical sound itself. . . . The plane on which we hear music without thinking, without considering it in any way"—and what I call "listening for plot," that is, listening for the way musical ideas are connected and strung together to create a purely musical "story." Though it is rarely done consciously, the creator of every work of art from the simplest popular entertainment to the most complex modernist poetry or avant-garde music embeds in its content a belief about the identity of its audience and what they will or will not be able to follow. Most often, the writer simply assumes sub-consciously that the audience will follow what the writer could fol-low himself. For example, the writers of television dramas like *CSI* and *Law & Order* presume that their audiences are capable of follow-ing and remembering plot developments throughout the course of an hour-long program. Each moment of the script makes sense only as part of a larger, developing story, and viewers retain and update infor-mation as a program proceeds. Writers can create plot twists, red her-rings, and surprise outcomes only because viewers do not understand each moment in isolation but as part of a whole. They group and remember events, have expectations that are fulfilled or defeated, and continually reinterpret the meaning of earlier details in light of later plot developments. A seemingly offhand comment made by a witness in the opening moments of a show may turn out to be the key lie that eventually implicates him as the murderer at the show's end.

Similarly, composers assume that listeners are capable of following and remembering musical plot developments throughout the course of a composition. Each moment of a Beethoven symphony or a Haydn string quartet ultimately makes sense only as part of a larger, develop-ing story, but the plot twists, red herrings, and surprise outcomes the notes contain can only unfold if listeners are hearing and understand-ing each moment not in isolation but as part of a whole. Like televi-sion dramas, music also requires audiences that group and remember events, have expectations that are fulfilled or defeated, and continu-ally reinterpret the meaning of earlier details in light of later plot developments, but most people are far less experienced at doing this with music than they are at doing this with words. Consequently, music is often heard as a succession of isolated, out-of-context moments, without reference to what comes before and after—an experience somewhat like watching each minute of a movie without reference to the rest of the film. Helping you learn to listen to a piece of music the way you watch a film will be one of the principal goals of this book.

A Plot by Haydn

Though I will look step-by-step at what is involved in listening for plot in the next several chapters, I want to use one brief example in this opening chapter as an introduction to the approach. (I will return to this excerpt and discuss it in greater detail in several upcoming chapters.) Here are the opening sixteen measures from the final movement of Franz Joseph Haydn's String Quartet, op. 76, no. 5.

EXAMPLE 1

The movement begins with a joke. The two chords that traditionally end a Classical period piece are wittily used as a beginning. The effect is like starting a film with the words "The End." The two and a half beats of silence that follow the opening two chords are as important as the chords themselves. They not only give you time to take in Haydn's witty gesture, to let the joke land, so to speak, but they give you time, if you are listening for plot, to wonder what Haydn could possibly be up to. Is this insignificant idea from the musical scrap heap really the opening idea? The movement's main character? By repeating the idea in measures 2 and 3, Haydn suggests that it is, and he continues the comedy by running three "The Ends" together without intervening pauses to make a kind of "combo package": The End, The End, The End.

What happens next goes to the heart of the difference between Copland's "listening on the sensuous plane" and listening for plot. This opening six-measure phrase (The End . . . The End . . . The End–The End–The End) is immediately followed by a completely unrelated idea: a folklike repeated-note accompaniment figure that continues underneath a lively tune played by the first violin, then by the cello. If you are listening casually, this second phrase offers the pleasure of hearing an energetic tune in two different instruments (violin and cello) and in two different registers (above and below the ticking accompaniment) but nothing more.

However, if you are an active listener, listening for plot, fifteen seconds into the piece your mind is already bursting with possibilities and questions. What was that first phrase all about? Are we supposed to take two chords repeated five times seriously as a theme, as a main character in the movement's story? Or was it simply a witty introduction never to be heard again, with the violin/cello tune of the second phrase being the "real" topic of the piece? Do the two phrases relate in any way? Will Haydn try to combine or connect them somehow? How do we make sense of their sequence? Are there little fragments or motives in the violin/cello melody that have potential for development? Above all, a participatory listener, like the viewer of a film, is on the edge of his seat, engaged by the key question at the heart of all plot-based listening: What will happen next?

We will follow the development of Haydn's intricate plot in the course of the next few chapters to see how it all turns out, but let's go back and begin to look in detail at how musical narratives are created, developed, and resolved. Since the proverbial journey of a thousand miles begins with a single step, let's start with the first step in any compelling plot—the beginning.

[2]

Beginnings Are
Everything

---

*The difficulty for me is beginning an opera, finding, that is, its
musical atmosphere. Once the beginning is fixed and composed,
there is nothing more to fear: the opera has been determined and
it goes.*

—GIACOMO PUCCINI

*A poem assumes direction with the first line
laid down.*

—ROBERT FROST

Beginnings matter. "It was the best of times, it was the worst
of times." "Lolita, light of my life, fire of my loins." Like great
first lines in literature, the opening measures of a piece can instantly
draw us in and create a musical environment with a particular style
of speech, tone, and vocabulary. Take the following well-known
openings.

In each case it takes no more than a few seconds for these pieces
to create their distinctive musical atmosphere. How do they do it?
What makes a great opening idea?

11

EXAMPLE 2

EXAMPLE 3

EXAMPLE 4

"Sticky" Ideas

In his book *The Tipping Point*, Malcolm Gladwell talks about how advertisers are always searching for "sticky" ideas, ideas or logos that will quickly "stick" in the public's mind and be easily remembered. For example, "Winston tastes good like a cigarette should," in which both the rhyme (good/should) and the incorrect grammar ("like," not "as") help make the phrase memorable. In a similar way, great musical openings are often generated by musically sticky ideas.

In a vocal work like George Frideric Handel's *Messiah*, a sticky idea is one that is not only musically memorable but also somehow manages to convey the essence of the text's meaning in just a few notes. The subtitle of Gladwell's book is *How Little Things Can Make a Big Difference*, and often the tiniest differences can turn an ordinary idea into an unforgettable one. If you take the four famous first notes of

Handel's "Hallelujah Chorus" and alter their rhythm so that every note lasts one beat, it would sound like this.

EXAMPLE 5

Hal - le - lu - jah

"Hallelujah," in this square, wooden version is utterly non-ecstatic. If we keep the rhythm of "Ha-le" but double the speed of "lu-jah," the idea becomes slightly more interesting but still is nothing special.

EXAMPLE 6

Hal - le - lu - jah

What makes it magic is Handel's lengthening of the first note. The sustained "Ha" grows in energy until it spills over into the excited, quicker-by-contrast "le-lu-jah" (with a fantastic syncopated "le"), and the four-note combination is classic Handel: musically memorable and a perfect depiction of the word's meaning.

EXAMPLE 7

Hal - le - lu - jah

It's Got Rhythm

Musical "stickiness" knows no genre boundaries. Though George and Ira Gershwin's "I Got Rhythm" might be less religious than Handel's *Messiah*, its opening is equally sticky, and the technique used by the two composers is remarkably similar. The song is defined by the fact that its main idea "has rhythm"—that is, it "swings"—and this highly distinctive rhythm dominates the piece. Once again, little things make a big difference. If we alter the first four notes of the Gershwins' opening the same way we altered Handel's so that every note lasts one beat, it would sound like this.

EXAMPLE 8

This boring version has no rhythm. If we give the idea *some* rhythm and make it somewhat better by syncopating it slightly, we could turn it into an almost-Gershwin version, which would sound like this.

EXAMPLE 9

What makes the Gershwins' version so fantastic is that unlike in these square versions, where each note lasts four quick, ordinary, sixteenth-note beats, in the real version each note lasts only three beats, making its syncopation unusual, surprising, and great. It has rhythm!

EXAMPLE 10

This catchy syncopated rhythm is the key to the entire song. The Gershwins use the same rhythm for the next lyric—"I got music." (Sing it to yourself.) And the next—"I got my man." (The B section is made out of the opening rhythm as well. Clap "Old man trouble," then "I don't mind him," then "You won't find him," and you'll see that they all have the identical rhythm of the opening idea.) But instead of finishing the opening phrase with the same rhythm one more time, the Gershwins give us the musical equivalent of a punch line. The only new rhythm in the phrase—eight notes for "Who could ask for anything more?"

EXAMPLE 11

It is not only rhythm, however, that makes this opening great. The pitches complement the rhythm in an amazing way. The song opens with four ascending notes: C–D–F–G. "I got music" uses the same four notes backward: G–F–D–C. Then it's back to the original version, C–D–F–G, for "I got my man." And then after nothing but the same four notes (C, D, F, and G) forward and backward for the first three lines of text, the notes, like the rhythm, change for "Who could ask for anything more?" They complete the plot.

Music without Words

Great openings are not limited to music with words, of course, and sticky beginnings are not only created by means of distinctive rhythms and melodies. Sometimes pure harmony, irrespective of melody or rhythm, can make an equally irresistible opening. Frédéric Chopin's *Nocturne in B Major*, for example, begins with a lush, beautiful chord, built up one note at a time. The chord's overtones, held by the piano's pedal, gloriously resonate, then die away for four beats until a second chord, almost prim in comparison, played all notes at once, resolves the opening gesture. This magical opening is a storyteller's beginning, a two-chord "Once upon a time" introduction whose rich harmony casts a spell that lures us into the world of the melody that follows.

EXAMPLE 12

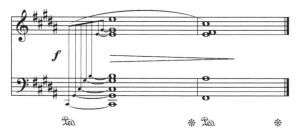

If Chopin's opening instantly creates a context of rich harmony, Antonio Vivaldi's "Spring" Concerto from his *Four Seasons* begins with the plainest harmony imaginable. Two measures of nothing but basic E-major chords. (Look at the bass line and you will see E's repeated over and over again.) Because Vivaldi's opening is so simple harmonically, the speeding up of the bass line and the three new quick chords in measure 3 make an enormous impact. They become, in the context of this opening, a significant event. And as in "I Got Rhythm," the melody perfectly complements the excitement caused by the new and faster harmony. The melody in the first two measures is played by the first violins, with the second violins clearly in an accompanying role. However, as the harmony speeds up and new chords are added, the second violins join the first violins in beautiful parallel motion and play the conclusion of the phrase with them at a slightly lower pitch, as if the solo melody had become a duet to close the thought. Though Vivaldi and Gershwin have completely different styles and vocabularies, their musical punch lines function in nearly identical ways.

EXAMPLE 13

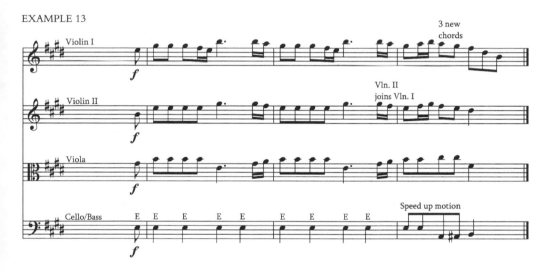

As you can already see from these few examples, there are as many different ways of beginning a piece of music as there are individuals, and each beginning requires something different from the listener. Each opening transports us into a world that has its own unique vocabulary. It might be the harmony that is distinctive, or the melody or rhythm. But it also might be the orchestration, as in the opening of Igor Stravinsky's *Petrushka*. Or the register, like the extremely low-pitched beginning of Henryk Górecki's Third Symphony. It might even be the tempo, like the glacially slow opening of Richard Wagner's *Tristan and Isolde*, in which each gesture (including the pauses between phrases) is stretched out and becomes almost surreally heightened. The piece's mythic timescale is established by the end of this first, slow-motion phase.

First Impressions

When you begin a conversation with someone you haven't met before, you quickly try to get a feel for how he speaks, for his basic vocabulary. The same is true when you encounter a new piece of music. Compositions, like individuals, tend to reveal a great deal about their personalities the moment they enter a room. However, though many pieces do in fact begin with catchy, attention-grabbing ideas like the ones we have been discussing, there are a whole group of utterly non-spectacular beginnings that make no attempt to seduce whatsoever. These openings not only do not make a dazzling first impression, their non-impressiveness is precisely their point, and they require a completely different kind of listening.

Take the opening of *The Art of the Fugue*—Johann Sebastian Bach's famous collection of fourteen fugues and four canons all based on this opening idea:

EXAMPLE 14

Half notes   Quarter notes   Tied note   Eighth notes

Though this theme does have some narrative drive—notice the way it gradually moves from slow notes to fast notes with the tied note in the middle of the phrase, avoiding mechanical squareness while making a subtle rhythmic climax—it is fundamentally *not* a flashy idea, nor is it designed to be. Bach deliberately chooses a theme that is plain enough to be subjected to the enormous variety of contrapuntal treatments it will receive in the course of his tour-de-force demonstration of fugal technique. (There are many other Bach fugues with non-catchy openings that function similarly.) Its meaning lies not in what it is, but in what it will become. When we hear the theme played at the opening of the first fugue, it is almost unimaginable that the next forty-five minutes of complex music could possibly be created out of its simple structure. Similarly, when we listen to the banal waltz tune by Anton Diabelli that opens Ludwig van Beethoven's *Diabelli Variations*, it seems equally inconceivable that the sublime music of the thirty-three variations could possibly be hidden in this trivial melody. Pieces like these make us ask, "How could this come from that?" Arnold Schoenberg said that Bach taught him "the art of creating the whole from a single kernel," and it is the dazzling difference between the whole (the entire *Art of the Fugue* and the entire *Diabelli Variations*) and the kernel (the *Art of the Fugue* theme and Diabelli's waltz tune) that is the essence of these pieces.

Beginnings like these, in which the meaning of an opening becomes clear only over time, often over the entire piece, take extraordinary compositional courage and a deep belief in an audience's intelligence. They ask the listener to do something that is almost inconceivable in today's fast-paced, hyperkinetic world: they ask the listener to wait.

It is important to understand just how radical and challenging that request is, yet how central it is to so much of classical music. Like other kinds of great art, great music asks us not to judge by first impressions, but rather to assume that the meaning of an idea is almost never immediately apparent. Only after a theme has been developed, varied, extended, and placed in multiple contexts over the course of an entire piece can we begin to grasp its sense. Even sticky beginnings like those of the "Hallelujah Chorus" and Vivaldi's "Spring" Concerto ask the listener to wait for their full meanings to be understood as their material is integrated into the ongoing narrative of the piece. These openings do more than just seize the listener's attention; they become part of the work's core material and are altered, developed, and transformed as the piece progresses.

The opening gestures of these pieces, like the events of our lives, acquire their meanings over time—as we see how things turn out, as "a single kernel" turns into "the whole." I mentioned in chapter 1 that every piece of music has embedded in its content a belief about the identity of its audience and what they will or will not be able to follow. Great music, like the music we have been looking at in this chapter, requires an audience that is willing to stay with the journey of a composition as significance and meaning accumulate. An audience that believes that first impressions and beginnings are only part of the story. An audience that is willing to wait. Beginnings may be everything—they matter enormously—but they are only the beginning.

[3]

Repetition

Contrast produces an immediate effect. Similarity satisfies us only in the long run. Contrast is an element of variety, but it divides our attention. Similarity is born of a striving for unity.

—IGOR STRAVINSKY

Now that we have looked at opening ideas in a preliminary way, let's look more closely at how composers construct musical phrases and the crucial role that repetition plays in structuring plots. Descriptive terminology can be notoriously problematic where music is concerned, as the pin-it-down rigidity of dictionary-style definitions is often fundamentally at odds with the variety and fluidity of musical speech, but in ascending order of length, here is how Grove's *Dictionary of Music* defines the three fundamental units of musical speech:

Motive: The shortest subdivision of a theme or phrase that still maintains its identity as an idea.

Phrase: A short musical unit of varied length . . . generally regarded as longer than a motive but shorter than a period.

Period: A musical statement terminated by a cadence. A period, however short or long, extends until its harmonic action has come to a close.

Though these definitions have value, I often find it more helpful to think of *motive*, *phrase*, and *period* as analogues for the three basic units of verbal speech: *word*, *clause*, and *sentence*. Taking the analogy one step further, there are as many different kinds of musical phrases as there are sentence types, and as many different ways of turning motives into phrases and periods as there are of turning words into clauses and sentences. This chapter focuses on one of the most important techniques composers use to construct meaningful, understandable, coherent sentences: repetition. (I will have much more to say about the role of repetition in creating large-scale form in later chapters.)

Exact Repeats

Repetition can operate at any level of structure—composers can repeat motives, phrases, or periods. (Like orators can repeat words, phrases, or sentences.) For the sake of clarity, we will refer to three different kinds of repeats: exact repeats, transposed repeats (repeats starting on a different note), and varied repeats. The Haydn string quartet opening we looked at in chapter 1 is a witty example of one of the simplest forms of repetition: a phrase built completely out of a single repeated motive. The motive ("The End" followed by two and a half beats of silence) is stated, repeated once identically, and then repeated three times with the silences removed. Though it might seem like academic hairsplitting, if we want to hear Haydn's plot the way he conceived it, it is important to realize that the motive is not just the notes, but rather the notes *plus* the silences that follow. Otherwise we will not hear the combination with the silences removed (The End–The End–The End) as a witty variation—an event in the plot. Though the listener cannot know it at this point in the piece, these silences will ultimately become as important to Haydn's plot as the notes themselves.

Transposed Repeats

Short phrases that are made up of exact repeats of a motive, like the one in the Haydn example, are relatively rare—Vivaldi's "Spring" Concerto (example 4) also repeats its opening phrase exactly, only more softly—but brief musical phrases built up out of transposed repeats are extremely common. The well-known opening of the "Fossils" movement from Camille Saint-Saëns's *Carnival of the Animals* is a clear example.

EXAMPLE 15

After a grunt in the strings startles us into attention, the xylophone begins with an inside joke: a five-note motive that is in fact the first five notes of the main theme of Saint-Saëns's own piece *Danse Macabre*—a witty musical "fossil," or fragment of a piece of "old" music. He then immediately repeats the five-note motive transposed lower, then a third time transposed still lower (with slightly larger intervals), ending the phrase seamlessly with a repeated-note idea. Three repetitions and an ending make for a clear, simple, "gettable" structure.

The opening phrase of Beethoven's Piano Sonata op. 109 works almost identically. This time, a short four-note, up-down motive is immediately transposed lower, followed by a third repeat transposed still lower which flows effortlessly to an ending.

EXAMPLE 16

The Saint-Saëns and Beethoven excerpts are incomplete sentences: the musical equivalent of introductory dependent clauses. The Saint-Saëns example is the first clause in a common two-part, question-and-answer, *antecedent-consequent* phrase structure in which repetition plays a central role. The first part of the clause (the antecedent) is open-ended. The second part (the consequent) resolves the phrase harmonically to complete the thought, in the case of "Fossils" by simply repeating the antecedent phrase (all three inner repeats) while altering the ending.

EXAMPLE 17

Notice that even in this simple example, repetition operates on more than one level of structure. Inner repetition of a five-note motive generates the antecedent phrase, while repetition of the entire antecedent phrase generates the consequent phrase.

Antecedent-consequent phrases like these are extremely common, particularly in the music of the Classical and Romantic periods, but they are also prevalent in folk and popular music, often in surprisingly subtle ways. The nursery rhyme "London Bridge Is Falling Down" begins with what seems to be a seven-note motive, "London Bridge is falling down." But then just the last three notes of the idea are repeated twice—"falling down," "falling down" (transposed lower, then back at the original level). The consequent phrase repeats the antecedent—"London Bridge is falling down"—but invents a new ending for the closing words, "my fair lady," to finish the phrase. (Notice how the graceful leaps in the notes for "my fair lady" beautifully contrast the rest of the stepwise melody to end the phrase.)

EXAMPLE 18

These repetition-based, antecedent-consequent phrases show up in twentieth-century music as well. In perhaps the clearest example imaginable of how little things can make a big difference, Leoš

Janáček's *Intimate Letters* quartet (1928) opens with an antecedent-consequent tune in which the consequent phrase repeats the entire antecedent phrase note-for-note but simply adds one extra note at the end (while getting slower and softer) to complete and resolve the thought.

EXAMPLE 19

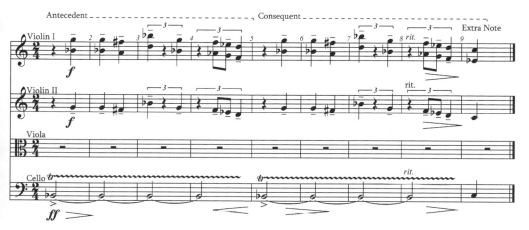

What Does It All Mean?

Having looked closely at these small-scale examples, let's see what they have to teach us at this point in our discussion about the function of repetition. To recapitulate, the Haydn string quartet example from chapter 1, which we looked at again in this chapter, begins with an ending turned into a beginning. After two and a half beats of silence, the opening gesture is repeated exactly. But though the notes are the same, their meaning is now completely different. In music (as in a lecture, a book, or a poem), repeating something lets us know that it matters. Repetition is a way of taking a motive or a phrase out of the ongoing musical stream and underlining it. Haydn's repeat tells us that this witty "ending turned into a beginning" is not just an isolated joke, but an idea that counts. Repetition, however, not only tells the listener that that something is significant, but it also clarifies the precise nature of that significance.

When Saint-Saëns repeats the five-note idea of "Fossils" the first time (example 15), he tells us that it matters. Transposing it a second time further confirms its importance. But when the consequent phrase repeats the entire first phrase and changes only the ending, it tells us that the opening idea is not one measure long but three measures long: not just the motive, but all three statements of the motive combined. And though I do not want to anticipate the material in chapter 6, "Forward-Backward Listening," when the next eight measures repeat this entire eight-measure phrase, we suddenly discover that the opening idea is neither a one-measure motive nor a three-measure, thrice-repeated version of this motive, but in fact the entire eight-measure, antecedent-consequent phrase. The unit of thought is continually enlarging. Repeating a whole block of music tells us that the entire block, not just a single segment, is the idea. Like taking a felt-tip marker and highlighting the key words in a sentence, repeating elements in music creates meaningful groupings, clarifies structure, and shows us what is important.

Though this kind of painstaking verbal description of the way repetition clarifies structure can seem dry and academic, hearing the technique in action, in the hands of a master like Haydn, is exhilarating, witty, and surprising. For the purpose of clarity at this early stage in our discussion, I have essentially been dealing only with the melody of each example and the way it is repeated. I have paid no real attention to anything about these melodies other than their pitches—not their rhythm, dynamics, articulations, or instrumentation—and I have completely ignored their harmony and accompaniments, preferring to save these topics for detailed consideration in later chapters. However, without wishing to get ahead of ourselves, I want to finish this chapter by looking at one extended example—still essentially one phrase, though now a three-clause, sixteen-measure phrase—to give you a more complete, three-dimensional picture of how repetition creates plot and clarifies meaning. Here are the first sixteen measures of the final movement of Haydn's C Major Piano Sonata H. 50.

EXAMPLE 20

A Dazzling, Summarizing Example

Though it is by no means obvious on a first listening, all fifteen suc-
ceeding measures of this excerpt are, amazingly enough, exact, transposed, or varied repeats of measure 1. In all of the previous examples
in this chapter, we have been treating the melody of each passage as
the musical "idea," but for Haydn the opening left-hand accompaniment (the four-note scale C–D–E–F in measures 1 and 2) is as much
of an idea as the right-hand "melody" (the three repeated C's in
measure 1).

There are two keys to understanding Haydn's plot in this opening.
First, we need to hear the right hand of measure 2 as a transposed and
varied repeat of the right hand of measure 1. In other words, the three
repeated notes (C–C–C) are transposed (D–D–D) and decorated by
a note above and a note below (eD–Dc–D). So instead of beginning
the piece with a straightforward transposition (C–C–C/D–D–D),
Haydn begins with a witty, varied transposition (C–C–C/eD–Dc–D).
Second, though the idea in the right hand in measures 4 and 5
(C–D–E–F) sounds new, it is in fact a repeat of the opening four-note
scale from the left hand of measure 1 (C–D–E–F). For extra credit,
notice that the left hand that accompanies this four-note ascending
scale in measures 4 and 5 is the same figure upside down. A four-note
descending scale! Yet another varied repeat of measure 1.

Haydn's ingenuity in the handling of these simple materials is dazzling, and once you can hear these two connections, you can follow the plot. I mentioned in chapter 1 that every piece of music is created with a belief about the identity of its audience and what they will or will not be able to follow. Music like this requires a highly intelligent, participatory, edge-of-the-seat listener, able to keep up with the astonishingly fast pace of Haydn's musical invention. Watch how quickly the thoughts develop. Haydn states the two germs of the piece in measure 1. By measure 2 he is already decorating the repeated-note idea in the right hand, and then that decorated version is transposed in measure 3 (remember, repetition lets us know an idea is an idea). Then the right hand comes in with its seemingly new idea in measures 4 and 5 (which we now know comes from the left hand of measure 1), and transposes it higher in measures 6 and 7 to let us know (through repetition) that it's an idea.

Now the fun begins in earnest, and our earlier discussions of repetition and plot begin to pay off. Until measure 7 we have been listening and understanding the plot of the piece in small units of one or two measures. Measure 1, then measures 2 and 3 as a group, measures 4 and 5, and measures 6 and 7. But when measure 8 starts to repeat the opening an octave higher, like a typical listener in Haydn's day who was familiar with antecedent-consequent phrases, we begin to have expectations—the kind of expectations that are the key to following the plot in a piece of music, a novel, or a television drama. We expect, as a knowledgeable listener in Haydn's day would have, the whole wonderfully irregular, seven-measure phrase to repeat intact with some slight alteration at the end to complete the thought. (Something like in "Fossils.") And for two measures, measures 8 and 9, we're right. Haydn does copy measures 1 and 2, giving us just enough repetition to lure us into his trap in measure 10: the essence of what makes Haydn great.

The right hand in measure 10 is "correct." Just as we are expecting, it is the right hand of measure 3. But the chord in the left hand is completely wrong! It sounds like a mistake, as if the pianist had simply played the wrong notes from the wrong key. And Haydn makes sure we cannot possibly miss it. The opening nine measures have been played softly (*piano*) but the "wrong-chord" measure is suddenly marked *forte* (loud), and the chord is followed by a dramatic, insouciant pause with a fermata—an indication that the performer is to hold the pause even longer than printed. Enough time to make sure the wrong notes "register" and the listener is appropriately shocked.

Having broken off the repeat after three measures, Haydn tries again, and starts to repeat from the beginning one more time. (Measures 12 and 13 repeat measures 1 and 2.) But when measure 14 again brings us to the famous third measure that stopped us dead in our tracks in measure 10, he gives us yet another left-hand version! A new plot twist. A subtly different chord with a new, rich color, held not for the whole measure as in measure 3 and measure 10, but now played three times. And as if that isn't enough, just as we're recovering from the shock, he adds two new transpositions of the idea to complete the thought, omitting our four-note scale idea entirely.

This is what listening for plot is all about: Listening for the way musical ideas are strung together to create a "story." Listening "from the inside out": from the composer's point of view. Noticing what Haydn wanted you to notice. Though it takes some time to verbally describe plots like these in detail, it is completely possible to hear them as they whiz by, once you learn how to listen for them. Stravinsky said that all composition is ultimately about balancing the demands of unity and variety, similarity and contrast. Too much similarity or repetition leads to boredom. Too much variety leads to chaos. Though it is hard to imagine a passage with more variety, contrast, and surprise than the opening of Haydn's C Major Piano Sonata, as we have just seen, it is utterly unified. Every measure is an exact, transposed, or varied repeat of measure 1. The passage is a perfect Stravinsky-like blend of unity and variety. Continually varied, yet completely unified. Shocking and surprising, yet somehow inevitable and right. It has an intricate plot worthy of a master, yet to follow it all you have to do is listen.

[4]

Comma, Semicolon, Period
The Meaning of Cadence

If I see an ending I can work backwards.

—ARTHUR MILLER

In chapter 3 we looked at the fundamental units of musical speech—motive, phrase, and period—as analogues for the fundamental units of verbal speech: word, clause, and phrase. In this chapter, we continue this grammatical analogy by looking at cadences as a musical form of punctuation. How do we know when a written sentence has ended? When we come to a period. How do we know when a musical sentence has ended? When we come to a cadence.

The *Harvard Dictionary of Music* defines the purely musical meaning of *cadence* as "A melodic or harmonic formula that occurs at the end of a section or a phrase conveying the impression of a momentary or permanent conclusion. Cadences are called 'weak' or 'strong' the more or less final the sensation they create." When most people think of the term *cadence*, they think of what musicians call a *perfect authentic cadence*, the two-chord ending, dominant–tonic, that we saw Haydn wittily turn into a beginning in chapter 1.

EXAMPLE 21

However, there are many different kinds of cadences, and they do far more than simply end musical sentences. Cadences play as important a role in organizing musical structure as punctuation plays in organizing sentence structure. Without punctuation, both written and musical speech would turn into extended run-on sentences, and learning to listen for cadences and how they structure musical flow is vital to understanding musical grammar.

Comma, Semicolon, Period

Written speech offers a variety of ways to indicate weaker and stronger interruptions in the flow of a sentence. A comma indicates a relatively weak pause, a semicolon a stronger pause, and a colon a still stronger pause, with dashes and parentheses offering other mid-sentence options. Though a period is the standard sentence-ending punctuation mark, a question mark or an exclamation point can be used to convey a different kind of final feeling. Musical speech offers even more options for indicating weaker and stronger pauses than written speech, and different historical periods and musical styles use completely different cadence formulas. If we include medieval and Renaissance music in the discussion, we face a bewildering array of labels: double-leading tone cadences, Phrygian cadences, Landini cadences, suspension cadences, and anticipation cadences in addition to the more familiar eighteenth- and nineteenth-century authentic cadences, half cadences, imperfect cadences, deceptive cadences, and plagal cadences.

The good news for anyone who is not a music theorist or a musicologist is that there is absolutely no need for you to learn all of these cadence forms and names. What is important is for you to become sensitive to what spawned all these labels in the first place—the many different ways composers have used cadences to create musical punctuation, regulate musical flow, and "convey the impression of a momentary or permanent conclusion." Let's start with the most familiar eighteenth- and nineteenth-century cadences to hear how composers distinguish between different degrees of musical finality—between musical commas, semicolons, and periods—and see how these distinctions organize musical structure.

Comma

Here is the opening orchestral section of "Autumn" from Vivaldi's *Four Seasons*.

EXAMPLE 22

[continued]

EXAMPLE 22 [continued]

The first cadence is in measure 3, and like the one at the end of the first half of our "Fossils" example in chapter 3 is traditionally called a half cadence. It is the musical equivalent of a comma, the weakest, or least final, form of cadence, and clearly requires another clause of music for any real sense of finality. Note however, that though the cadence is inconclusive, the entire phrase is designed to lead to it and make it the "main event" of this opening sentence. The melody of measure 1, which is repeated in measure 2 (showing us that it is an idea), contains only two notes, A and B-flat, and these two notes are always harmonized by the same two basic chords. Much like the opening of "Spring," which we looked at in chapter 2, the simplicity of this beginning makes the arrival of a new melody note in measure 3 (a G), accompanied by new, quick-changing chords that push to the cadence, a significant event. Listen to the example again and notice, even in this simple context, Vivaldi's characteristic drive to the cadence. This cadence is more than just a mere punctuation mark providing a "momentary conclusion" to the phrase. Its meaning is inextricably bound up with the plot of the phrase as a whole. The cadence is given its sense of finality by the way the phrase moves toward it, while as end point and goal it gives meaning and shape to the entire phrase that precedes it. In much the same way, the daily noon-hour lunch break in a factory worker's schedule not only marks a dividing point in the workday, but it also gives a direction to the hours from nine to twelve that push toward the lunch break—the day's main structural event. (And the hours from nine to twelve usually have their own structure determined by "weaker cadences"—ten-minute coffee breaks.)

Semicolon/Period

As I mentioned earlier, it is not important as a listener that you be able to name the cadences you hear in music, but it is important that you be sensitive to how "final" they feel. If the half cadence in measure 3 is a musical comma, the stronger cadence that occurs in measure 11 is a kind of musical semicolon. This time the music resolves firmly to our home F-major chord, the central chord of the piece, but the resolution in the melody, to an A rather than an F, is not as final as it could be. (The sound is what is important, not the labels or names of notes.) Two measures later, however, the identical cadence figure returns an octave lower, and this time resolves the melody to an F, ending the entire opening section with a strong and final musical period.

There are two main points I want you to be aware of in this passage. First, listen to it again in its entirety and try to hear the different degrees of finality of the four cadences—musical commas in measures 3 and 6, a semicolon in measure 11, and a period in measure 13. Second, notice how these four cadences literally structure the entire opening, with each cadence clearly demarcating a gradual movement from something open-ended to something final: from comma, to semicolon, to period.

Deception and Delay

Because perfect authentic cadences are so final and convey an "impression of permanent conclusion" so strongly, composers frequently postpone their arrival to make them even more emphatic. In "Autumn," Vivaldi delays his final section-ending cadence by preceding it with a slightly weaker cadence in which the melody avoids the tonic note. In his Piano Sonata in B-flat Major K. 333 (315c) (example 23), Wolfgang Amadeus Mozart subtly delays his section-ending cadence in measure 10 with two weaker, comma-like cadences, one in measure 6 and one in measure 8. In each of these cadences, the bass note (a D, not a B-flat) avoids the tonic note, making the cadence feel less final and less rooted. Delaying final resolution strengthens the cadence that ultimately ends the section and makes it feel even more conclusive.

In the same way that punctuation marks structure the flow of a written sentence, these cadences structure the flow of Mozart's musical sentence. When the music refuses to resolve definitively at the first cadence, in measure 6, the motion speeds up. Mozart's second try has more urgency. Measure 7 is a more intense version of measure 5, and the scale in measure 8 has enormous sweep compared to the scale in measure 6, leading to a powerful resolution at the final cadence, with the highest notes of the piece so far, at the loudest dynamic (*forte*), with double notes in the right hand. Once again, the cadence is given meaning by the way the section moves toward it, while this final cadence, as end point and goal, gives meaning and shape to the entire section that precedes it.

EXAMPLE 23

Cadences as powerfully final as the ones that end our Vivaldi and Mozart examples can have an enormous impact on the structure of a composition. In many Baroque pieces, where the musical flow tends to be continuous once a composition is under way, these cadence points, and the sense of arrival and "momentary conclusion" they provide, can literally determine the architecture of an entire piece. In Bach's D Minor Two-part Invention, for example, three clearly audible, perfect authentic cadences—one in F major (measure 18), one in A minor (measure 38), and a final one in the home key of D minor in the last measure—organize the musical flow and define the structure of the whole composition. Each cadence point is the goal that its section heads toward and the first two cadences are also departure points for the new section that follows. This kind of overlap (a musical equivalent to enjambment in poetry), in which a cadence simultaneously ends one phrase while beginning the next, is one of the central ways composers create punctuation in musical sentences while still maintaining flow and continuity. A new melody begins at the same moment the harmony resolves. While the harmony goes "The End," a new melody starts above "End."

For Bach, these intermediate cadences are stopping points on a journey home to D minor. They function in Bach's narrative like Odysseus's sojourns at Circe's island, Calypso's island, and the Palace of Alcinous on his journey home to Ithaca. Because the invention's final D-minor cadence is the fundamental goal and destination of the entire piece (Bach's "Ithaca"), a dramatic extra cadence in measure 49, at what seems to be the moment of final resolution, is added. This is called a *deceptive cadence* because a chord is "deceptively" substituted for the expected D-minor chord, thereby making the actual cadence three measures later even more emphatic, satisfying, and final.

Once again, it is not learning the label "deceptive cadence" that is really important here, but rather that you hear the way a defining moment of musical punctuation—a final cadence—becomes more powerful through delay. Making musical events of various kinds more significant by delaying their arrival will be a topic we return to several times in this book, and as we shall see, scarcity not only increases the value of precious metals and natural resources, but it increases the value of musical resources, like a final tonic chord, as well.

EXAMPLE 24

Cadence in F major

Cadence in a minor

[continued]

EXAMPLE 24 [continued]

Deceptive cadence   Cadence in D major

One Hundred Years Later

It is, of course, not only music of the Baroque period that uses cadences to shape the structure of a piece. In a completely different musical style, with an updated harmonic language, Chopin's E Minor Prelude from his 24 Preludes op. 28 functions almost identically to Bach's invention, and neatly sums up nearly all of the points discussed in this chapter so far. On the most fundamental harmonic level, the entire prelude (one of the "Five Easy Pieces" played by Jack Nicholson's character in the movie of the same name) is ultimately about getting to a decisive, final cadence on the piece's home chord in its strongest form—an E-minor chord with an E in the bass. Like Bach's invention, Chopin's prelude only reaches its goal on the last chord of the piece, and the journey toward this chord structures the entire composition.

EXAMPLE 25

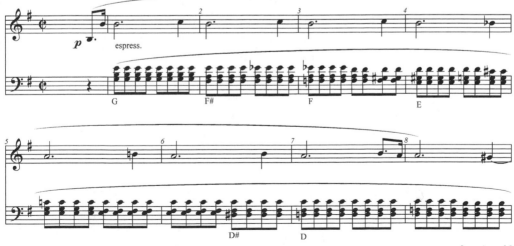

[continued]

EXAMPLE 25 [continued]

As we have already seen in chapter 1, a perfect authentic cadence ("The End") is made up of two chords: a dominant chord ("The") and a tonic chord ("End"). In the key of Chopin's prelude, those two chords are a B chord and an E-minor chord. (Non-musicians should think of these names as labels and listen for their sound. Don't worry about their technical makeup.) The entire first half of Chopin's prelude, measures 1 through 12, is a gradual descent in the left hand toward "The"—a B chord. Though the passage's heartbreaking, poignant chords seem to wander from key to key in an almost improvisatory fashion, if you listen closely to the bass line (the lowest left-hand notes), you can hear it move inexorably downward, always in the same eighth-note rhythm, step-by-step from the opening G down to B (G–F♯–F–E–D♯–D–C–B). The moment of arrival at measure 12 is clearly marked by the pause in the left hand and the elaborate decoration in the right hand, but though we have reached the dominant chord, the resolution to the tonic chord in measure 13 is not final. As in our Mozart example, it doesn't include the tonic note (an E) in the bass, but rather a G. Remember, hearing the different degrees of finality of cadences—how conclusive or inconclusive they feel—is the point here. The inconclusiveness of this cadence keeps the plot going.

Measure 13 starts to repeat the opening, and, having read about antecedent-consequent phrases in chapter 3, we suddenly realize that, for Chopin, the entire first twelve measures are a single unit. Though the chords and the bass line of the second phrase are an exquisite variation of the first phrase, the second phrase also moves step-by-step in the left hand from G down to B (measures 13 through 17). Having reached our dominant chord a second time, we are now ready for final resolution, and Chopin spends four full measures (measures 17 through 20) preparing us for this defining moment. But as in Bach's invention, instead of a resolution in measure 21 to E minor, we get a deceptive cadence. The three following measures take us to an utterly confusing, harmonically ambiguous pause in measure 23, where the piece simply stops dead. Just when it seems as if we will never find our way home to E minor, we finally get the cadence that we have been waiting for. With an almost surreal, textbook clarity and firmness, we finish with The End. The only perfect, authentic cadence in this entire prelude is saved till its very last measure.

Contemporary Music

I mentioned earlier that different historical periods and musical styles use completely different cadence formulas. One of the most important first steps for a listener encountering a new musical language is to get a feel for its cadences and punctuation, and this can be particularly challenging when dealing with twentieth- and twenty-first-century music. Mainstream concertgoers are generally familiar with the sound of the standard eighteenth- and nineteenth-century cadences even if they don't know their exact names or grammatical makeup. However, in later music, there is an enormous variety of musical styles and few conventional, standardized cadential formulas. Composers have created their own forms of punctuation, which listeners must try to grasp piece by piece, often on a single hearing.

Though there are far too many unique cadence forms in twentieth- and twenty-first-century music to generalize meaningfully about all of them, looking at a few brief examples of certain tendencies and recurring procedures can help train your ear and increase your ability to make sense of the many different kinds of musical punctuation this repertoire has to offer.

It is interesting that as twentieth-century composers began to invent sounds, colors, and harmonies unheard of in earlier music, they frequently held on in various ways to cadences from the past. The opening of the third movement of Maurice Ravel's Piano Concerto, for example, is an almost literal updating of our Haydn string quartet opening from chapter 1 that wittily turned an ending into a beginning. The bass line of measures 3 and 4 has the same notes as a "The End" cadence would have had in a G-major Haydn string quartet, D–G, though the solo G (plus bass drum!) is humorously delayed until after the chord is played. However, both of the chords above this traditional bass line have extra notes dressing up an old Haydnesque cadence in modern clothes and giving it a fresh, contemporary feel.

EXAMPLE 26

Stravinsky dresses up the identical final cadence, in the same key, with different added notes to wittily begin *The Soldier's Tale*. The first two dissonant measures make the mock-traditional cadence in measure 3 sound as if it is in quotation marks—a found object from the past, updated then inserted into Stravinsky's neoclassical canvas.

EXAMPLE 27

Composers like Dmitri Shostakovich and Sergei Prokofiev frequently use decorated versions of "The End" to provide grounding and resolution at the end of harmonically ambiguous passages like this one from Prokofiev's *Peter and the Wolf*.

EXAMPLE 28

Notice as you listen to this example the way the cadence at the end seems to clarify an otherwise confusing passage. Also notice that though the harmonic direction of the phrase seems unclear until the cadence, what gives it direction is the melody line, which ascends a half step at a time, ultimately from C to C. (A half step is the smallest distance possible on a piano between notes, the distance from any key to the next-nearest key, black or white.)

Many twentieth-century cadences keep the fundamental two-chord feeling and shape of "The End," but change both the bass line and the chords above it. In the Sarabande from Ravel's *Pour le Piano*, all of the chords in this final passage are non-traditional, built up with fourths, not the traditional thirds of tonal harmony. (Again, listen to the sound of these chords without worrying about their technical makeup.) Consequently, when we get to the penultimate chord of the movement ("The"), we do not have the normal expectations we have in a conventional cadence. We simply don't know where the chord will resolve, but if we had to guess we would probably guess E major. When instead it resolves incredibly softly (*pianissimo*) to C♯ minor, the one traditional triad in the passage, it is a complete, though subtle, shock. Ravel creates his own unique, elegant, modal cadence that although utterly unexpected, sounds, in retrospect, completely inevitable. A dance form (the sarabande) and a cadence from the past are filtered through Ravel's twentieth-century sensibility and emerge reinvented and new.

EXAMPLE 29

Atonal Music

Composers as diverse as Ravel, Shostakovich, Stravinsky, Benjamin Britten, Copland, and Béla Bartók created an entire repertoire of cadences like these that update traditional tonal formulas and infuse them with new life. However, some of the most interesting and challenging cadences for composer and listener alike are those designed to provide punctuation in contexts where the musical language is not tonal in any traditional sense. In the absence of conventional harmonic kinds of resolution, composers have had to find other ways of distinguishing between "momentary" and "permanent" conclusions. Often, it is pure gesture alone that lets us know a phrase has ended. The opening movement of Stravinsky's twelve-tone composition *Requiem Canticles*, for example, arrives at the final cadence by brute force. The same dissonant chord is simply repeated thirty-one times in constantly shifting rhythmic patterns, and then after a short pause played one more time with a sharp accent. This final accented chord ends the piece, though there is no harmonic resolution, no change of chords, and no cadence in any traditional sense. The piece ends because Stravinsky says it does. We know it is over because there is no more music.

EXAMPLE 30

With equal will, though in less aggressive fashion, Anton von Webern essentially does just the opposite in the third movement of his atonal *Six Pieces for Orchestra*. He simply sustains a dissonant chord (measure 4) and allows it to die away until the listener has no choice but to accept the chord, dissonant though it may be, as a cadence— a "momentary conclusion." (I will have much more to say about these kinds of endings in the final chapter, "Finished versus Complete.")

EXAMPLE 31

There is one more aspect of this passage that is relevant to a great deal of other contemporary music. Notice that after the cadence on the sustained chord in measure 4, the music picks up and starts a completely new musical idea, played by new instruments, in a new tempo, a new meter, and a new register. This complete contrast makes it clear *retrospectively* that the previous sustained chord has ended something. Very often in contemporary music a cadence is defined by the next music's being different. Starting something new can let the listener know that we have finished the preceding phrase or section. Even if that something new is actually nothing—that is, a rest. In the first movement of *Requiem Canticles*, for example, several short phrases end with a measure of silence, and it is this silent measure that functions each time as a cadence and lets us know the phrase has ended. Similarly, in the minimalist music of Steve Reich, a single chord often lasts three to four minutes, and in the magical moment when the chord finally changes, we realize that the previous section has finished.

Cadere: To Fall

There are as many different kinds of cadences in contemporary music as there are composers, but before we conclude this chapter it seems appropriate, since it is the source of the term *cadence* itself, to glance quickly at punctuation and cadence in a kind of music that for many listeners is as foreign as contemporary music: medieval music. The word *cadence* actually comes from the Latin verb *cadere*, "to fall," which referred to the way cadences were ordinarily made in the single-line world of medieval plainchant: by descending, or "falling," to the final note.

EXAMPLE 32

Tes - te___ Da - vid___ cum Si - bil - la

Though the musical possibilities in this single-line universe of plainchant might seem to be limited, the subtle, varied, and deeply expressive use of cadences in this repertoire is extraordinary. The first five clauses of the beautiful Gregorian chant "Ave María," have five different cadences that are "more or less final," "weaker or stronger," and "convey the impression of a more or less permanent conclusion" in the language of this single-line world with as much variety as the Bach, Vivaldi, and Mozart cadences we looked at earlier.

EXAMPLE 33

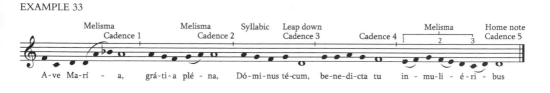

The opening invocation, "Ave María" ("Hail Mary"), literally "hails" Mary and calls us to attention with two striking leaps—a leap down on "Ave," which prepares the huge (in the context of this spare, mostly stepwise melody) leap up, from D to A, on "rí" of "María." Once you are inside this ancient musical language, the cadence is extraordinarily expressive. A simpler, more regular, and far less beautiful version might use one note for every syllable, like this: A–ve Ma–rí–a.

EXAMPLE 34

Compare my version to the example, which instead of simply leaping up to the high note to end the phrase, prepares the cadence with three notes on "rí" to gradually ease us into the cadence. This three-note melisma (singing more than one note on a single syllable is called a *melisma*) with its poignant half step movingly conveys in restrained fashion the emotion of the devout toward the Virgin Mary, while the extra, slightly higher decorative note "falls" to the cadence with a sigh. This cadence, though in a completely different style, is as inconclusive as Vivaldi's opening cadence and similarly requires additional music for resolution. In the grammar of plainchant, it is a musical semicolon.

The second clause, "grátia pléna" ("full of grace"), is even less conclusive. A two-note melisma on "plé" eases us into the cadence, but we are still up "high" in pitch on our A, and the phrase lacks any kind of conclusive "fall" or descent into the cadence on "na." This "momentary conclusion" is at most a musical comma.

The third cadence, on "Dóminus técum" ("God is with thee"), is striking. The vocal line is completely syllabic—five syllables, five notes—and the music literally "falls" into the cadence with a remarkable leap down of a fourth. Up to this point, the chant has gone from a seven-note phrase with one melisma to a six-note phrase with one melisma. This five-note phrase without a melisma—the most compressed and concentrated phrase so far—perfectly prepares the beautiful "benedicta tu in muliéribus" ("blessed art thou among women"). In the Latin sense of *cadere*, "to fall," this long phrase cadences, or "falls," gradually over fourteen notes to the home note, D. Its graceful descent is clear even visually. Everything contributes to the sense of arrival at the cadence. The phrase begins syllabically with "benedicta tu," but then three two-note-per-syllable/one-note-per-syllable pairs ("i-n mu . . . l-i é . . . r-i bus") ease us rhythmically into the cadence, and the arrival at D (on the syllable "é") is stabilized and made more conclusive by the two D's that follow.

Cadences

As we have seen, how composers punctuate their musical sentences has changed greatly over time. The techniques and cadences we find in the single-line world of plainchant are completely different from those we might find in a string quartet by Haydn, which are different from those we might find in a string quartet by Elliot Carter, or a symphonic work by György Ligeti, yet no matter the style or time period, musical sentences, like written sentences, require punctuation. Cadences are crucial because they demarcate events and provide landmarks that give structure to music, and this need to create structure seems to be an essential human trait operating outside of music as well. It was the original impulse behind the creation of the church calendar, which took a series of undifferentiated days and constructed a meaningfully punctuated year organized around two principal "cadences," or feasts: the Nativity and Easter. The liturgical year leads to these pivotal events like a phrase leads to a cadence. Even our secular year (particularly the retail component) organizes itself around cadential landmarks—Labor Day, Halloween, Thanksgiving, Christmas, et cetera—with the periods preceding these holidays defined in relationship to each upcoming celebration. We also have personal structural markers that function like cadences. Baptisms, bar mitzvahs, confirmations, graduations, weddings, silver and gold wedding anniversaries, reunions, and the like. These cadences function much as they do in music, to structure and shape the flow of our lives. Not all endings, personally or musically, are of the same finality—finishing freshman year (a half cadence) is not the same thing as graduating from college (a perfect authentic cadence). Yet all of these endings give a rhythm and a shape to our experience, and learning to listen for that shape, in music as in life, starts with cadences.

[5]

Compared-to-What Listening

It is insufficient merely to hear music in terms of the separate moments at which it exists. You must be able to relate what you hear at any given moment to what has just happened before and what is about to come afterward.

—AARON COPLAND

Up to this point in the book, we have kept our microscope trained on very small segments of music that are fundamentally no more than a single phrase in length. As we widen our lens in this chapter and focus our attention on the way composers combine phrases into sections and turn musical sentences into musical paragraphs, we begin to enter the domain of what I call "compared-to-what" listening.

I mentioned in chapter 1 that listening for plot involves listening for the way musical ideas are connected and strung together to create a "story"—hearing a piece of music not as a succession of isolated moments but as part of a whole. I pointed out that we routinely watch films in which each moment of the script only makes sense as part of a larger, developing story, and we retain and update plot developments as the film proceeds, comparing each moment to what came before and what comes after. What would it be like to listen to a piece of music the way we watch a film, hearing each moment in a continually evolving context?

Compared-to-What Mozart

Let's start to get a feel for this, still within a single phrase, by looking at a very simple example that we have already discussed. If you listen once again to the Mozart passage from chapter 4 (example 23), you might notice a lovely little detail in the fourth measure. For one split second (two notes), Mozart adds a second voice to the right hand, making a fluid, graceful ending to the first clause. But "fluid and graceful" *compared to what*? To be pedantically precise, compared to the three previous measures, in which the right hand plays only a single-line melody. The two beats of double notes are not lovely in and of themselves. If the right hand had played double notes for all four measures, there would be absolutely nothing special about these two beats at all. They are beautiful only in comparison to the single-line melody of the previous measures. They are beautiful only when they are heard in context.

Similarly, the scale in measure 8 that I described as having "enormous sweep" has enormous sweep only if heard, as Mozart intended, not in isolation but in comparison to the narrow range of the scale in measure 6. The identical notes of measure 8 in the context of a passage with swooping scales continually running up and down the keyboard would have no effect whatsoever. Finally, the cadence that ends the passage, with its crescendo to *forte*, high right hand, and two full measures of double notes, makes its impact only when heard in comparison to the range, dynamics, and textures of the whole preceding passage. Put simply, loud is loud, high is high, and thick is thick only in a particular context, and it is our sensitivity to Mozart's continually changing contexts of rhythm, dynamics, texture, and range that determines how much of this exquisite detail we notice.

If we were to go back and look again at all of the examples in the preceding chapters, we would discover that every plot element in these short single-phrases is dependent on a context for its meaning. None of these moments makes sense in isolation. The entire concept of a consequent phrase, for example, is obviously meaningless except in the context of an antecedent phrase. Haydn's *forte*, "wrong-note" chord in example 20 is only surprising in the context of the harmony and dynamics of the preceding phrase. However, as important as context is in these short, single-phrase examples, it is when composers start to combine phrases into sections, and turn musical sentences into musical paragraphs, that the true importance, richness, and complexity of compared-to-what listening becomes clear.

Compared-to-What Haydn: From Phrase to Section

Let's add two more phrases to the Haydn string quartet opening we looked at in chapter 1 and follow out this rich plot.

EXAMPLE 35

[continued]

EXAMPLE 35 [continued]

We have already seen how Haydn creates this witty beginning out of an ending. The opening idea, "The End" plus two and a half beats of silence, is repeated, then followed by the "combo package": three statements of "The End" run together without intervening pauses. Then, without any explanation, the next phrase suddenly leaves the opening idea behind and continues with a completely unrelated idea: a folklike repeated-note accompaniment figure underneath a lively tune played by the first violin then by the cello. This is followed by a quintessential compared-to-what moment. Without warning, in measures 17 through 20, our opening idea returns. If you are not listening closely, or more important, if you are not listening with an awareness of the context, this could easily sound like an exact repeat of the opening. Once again we hear the "The End plus silence" idea twice, followed by the combo package. However, two-thirds of the pauses have been wittily eliminated. "The End *pause-pause-pause*, The End *pause-pause-pause*" has been shortened to "The End *pause*, The End *pause*." Haydn's original six-measure idea, the basic unit of the piece, has been shortened to a four-measure idea, not by changing the notes, but by changing the silences or pauses surrounding the notes. This change, compressing the six-measure idea into four measures, *is* Haydn's point. To answer Anne, the radio listener I mentioned in chapter 1, it *is* the plot. And it is a plot told with nothing but notes. But the plot works only if the listener is comparing the second version to the first and noticing the difference. This does not mean that the listener must be able to articulate or explain the difference in any way. No mental calculation or analysis is necessary. All you have to do is listen, be aware of the difference, and notice it.

I have mentioned several times that the composer of every piece of music embeds in its content a belief about the identity of its audience and what they will or will not be able to follow. In his music, Haydn not only assumes that his audience will be able to keep up with the speed of his musical thought, he also assumes that they will be able to keep up with his constantly shifting compared-to-what contexts. He began the movement with a six-measure version of the opening idea. The second version (measures 17 through 20) took this unit and varied it by removing pauses. Before we even have time to finish processing this new version, Haydn immediately varies it again. Let's look closely at how this works, since it goes to the heart of how the meaning of a musical idea changes as a piece evolves.

We have already seen that the second version of our opening idea altered the pauses between the notes. The actual notes themselves, however, remained the same. Both versions repeated the identical two chords—"The End"—five times. In measure 20, Haydn begins a *third* version of the opening, transposing the second version (starting it on a lower note) and shifting it into a minor key. For most composers, this would be more than enough compositional activity for one phrase, but for Haydn it is just the beginning. It is simply astonishing how many possibilities Haydn hears in this simple idea. If he had merely copied the second version lower and in a minor key, it would have sounded like this.

EXAMPLE 36

But Haydn copies only as much as is necessary to lure the listener into his compared-to-what trap. He gets through "The End *pause*, The End *pause*," but then instead of finishing the phrase with the same chords (The End–The End–The End), he humorously transposes the combo package lower and puts it back in a major key.

Let's step back for a moment and look at what all of this detail means in terms of compared-to-what listening. There are three different versions of our opening idea in this passage. They are all reasonably similar, and if you are listening casually, on Copland's "sensuous plane," you might well think all three versions were the same. If you were particularly distracted, you might not even notice that the three versions were related at all. In that case, your reaction to each version would be limited to enjoying the general energy level of the music at that moment, and in the hands of excellent performers that can be quite entertaining. Regrettably, however, you would be missing the essence of Haydn's compared-to-what art, the essence of what makes Haydn great. Haydn not only assumed that you would compare the second version of the opening to the first one and "get" the witty compression, he also assumed that you would compare the third version to the second one and thoroughly enjoy the surprise when it didn't continue as expected. Music like this requires that kind of participatory audience for it to be fully successful. Without a compared-to-what listener hearing each moment as part of the whole, Haydn's sophisticated quartet becomes a tree falling in the forest with no one around to hear it.

If this seems daunting in any way, I want to emphasize once again that all you have to do is listen. Though this kind of musical plot can sound complicated when described in words, once you understand how it works, it is not at all difficult to hear. All that is really required is that you pay attention. I have played this string quartet for a wide variety of listeners, many with virtually no prior experience with classical music at all—inner-city schoolkids, doctors, employees at a utility company, executives at a major American corporation, and twenty-something computer types—and have invariably found that they were able to hear how these three versions were put together and notice the differences between them with barely any explanation. I might also add that the difference between their engagement with the music when they "got" what Haydn was up to and when they didn't was palpable. It was as if a foreign film had suddenly been translated into English.

One Hundred Years Later It's Still Compared-to-What

Once you begin to get familiar with the concept of compared-to-what listening, you will be able to apply it everywhere. More than a hundred years after Haydn wrote his quartet, Janáček constructed the opening three phrases of his *Intimate Letters* string quartet in an almost identical compared-to-what fashion.

EXAMPLE 37

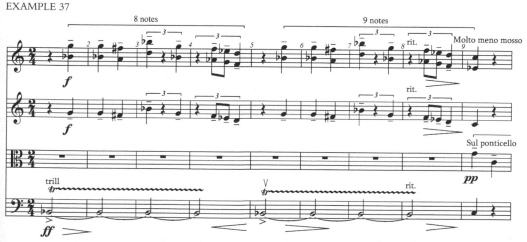

[continued]

EXAMPLE 37 [continued]

The quartet's title, *Intimate Letters*, refers to the more than seven hundred letters Janáček wrote to Kamilla Stösslová, his end-of-life muse, during the twelve years of their extraordinary relationship, and the piece's highly intense, emotional atmosphere is clear from the very first measure. The piece begins without preamble or introduction, and the opening idea we looked at briefly in chapter 3 is classic Janáček—a short, emotionally intense musical fragment with a passionate, surging energy generated by the intense trill in the cello and the spasmodic, irregular rhythm in the violins in measures 3 and 4 and 7 and 8. This is "idea as passionate outburst," only as long as it needs to be, a pithy utterance, then we move on. For future reference, note that the antecedent phrase has eight notes, followed by a consequent phrase that repeats these eight notes and adds one more to close.

Just as in Haydn's quartet, without any explanation, the next phrase abruptly leaves the opening idea behind and continues with a completely unrelated idea—an eerie viola solo, in a much slower tempo, played toward the bridge of the instrument (*sul ponticello*) for maximum strangeness. Janáček poetically describes this idea as "the effect of seeing Kamilla for the first time, the earth trembling." Though utterly different from the opening idea in sound, mood, and tempo, the viola solo is also a short, pithy utterance, repeated with an alteration at the end. We have no more idea what Janáček means by juxtaposing these two completely unrelated ideas then we did with Haydn, but Janáček, like Haydn, immediately returns to his opening idea to continue his plot.

As with our Haydn example, if you are not listening in compared-to-what fashion, this second version could easily sound like an exact repeat of the opening. We again have our intense trill (now transposed a step higher and in the viola instead of the cello) below our irregular melody in the violins (also transposed). But like Haydn, Janáček compresses this second version. Not, however, by removing pauses, but by removing notes. He starts by reducing the original eight-note idea to its first five notes, and then shortens the consequent phrase to only four. It is as if he is trying to strip away whatever is incidental in order to reduce the theme to its core essence. As we saw in chapter 3, repetition clarifies structure and shows us what matters. But only if we are comparing the compressed version with the original. Janáček compressing his eight-note idea to a four-note idea *is* the point. It *is* the plot.

Compared-to-What Debussy: The Art of Reharmonization

Compared-to-what listening will be a topic we return to in several different contexts later in this book, but there are two more aspects of it that require comment at this point. Though both the Haydn and Janáček examples dealt with listening this way in the realm of melody, there is an entire repertoire of musical examples that grow directly out its application to the realm of harmony through the use of a compositional technique called *reharmonization* (which simply means changing the chords underneath a melody or motive that repeats). Claude Debussy was a master of the technique, and his famous piano prelude "Footsteps in the Snow" is an exquisitely subtle and beautiful example. Here are the first two phrases.

EXAMPLE 38

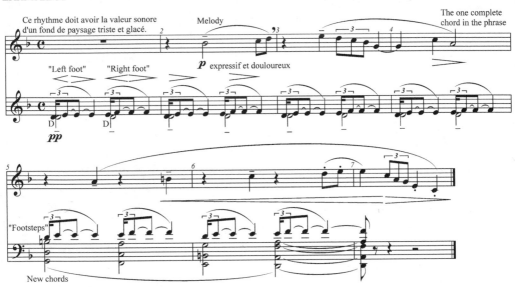

If you look at the printed score, you can get a sense of the subtle poetry of Debussy's aesthetic before you hear a single note simply by reading the evocative expressive indication underneath the opening rhythm: *"Ce rhythme doit avoir la valeur sonore d'un fond de paysage triste et glacé"* ("This rhythm must have the sonorous value of a sad and frozen landscape"). Debussy's subtlety shows up in every aspect of this music. The entire dynamic range of the piece extends from *pianississimo* (*ppp*) to *piano* (*p*)—from incredibly soft to soft. Though it is at first somewhat difficult to hear, there are two subtly distinct musical layers in the left hand at the opening. The "footsteps" motive, the upper line (D–E, E–F), is actually a separate layer from the repeated bass note underneath. There are two "footsteps," D–E and E–F, a left foot and a right foot if you will, with the second footstep starting where the first one left off. The piece as a whole is quietly revolutionary, and part of its quiet revolution is its quiet obsession. Not only do twenty-five of the thirty-six measures of the piece contain these two footsteps, but Debussy also repeats them forty-eight times without ever changing their notes. D–E, E–F, forty-eight times! How do you make a piece out of this, and what does it have to do with comparative listening?

In the first phrase (measures 1 through 4), the left hand repeats the two footsteps four times, always with the same bass note, D, underneath. Above this static, austere, two-part left hand, the right hand adds a third layer, a "melody" that elegantly fits in the rhythmic spaces left by the footsteps and only fully coincides with them at the end of the phrase when the two hands combine to make the one complete chord in the phrase. (Throughout his life, Debussy was accused of abolishing melody. Critics complained that his operas didn't sing, that no one could whistle his tunes, yet in the evocative, spare atmosphere of "Footsteps in the Snow," this simple ascending right-hand line is as "expressive and painful"—Debussy's marking—as any melody. Debussy did not abolish melody; he simply created a new kind.)

The second phrase (measures 5 through 7) is compared-to-what harmony in all its glory. The obsessive footsteps continue with two more pairs. But now Debussy replaces the spare, ascetic, repeated note underneath with four rich, exquisitely beautiful new chords. Though these chords are beautiful in and of themselves, it is the comparison with the austere first version that makes them so moving. Debussy's rich reharmonization of the footsteps motive completely alters the mood of the piece. A chilly gray landscape suddenly develops unexpected warmth and color.

The term *reharmonization* has the concept of "compared-to-what" built into its very grammar. *Re*-harmonizing a motive or a melody implies taking an original harmonization and revising it. The whole point is for the listener to compare the different versions, to hear the motive or the melody from a completely different perspective. The reharmonization of the footsteps in this second phrase changes our understanding of the motive by showing us another side of its character. Were we to listen to the rest of the piece, we would see that this second phrase is just the beginning. Every new statement of the footsteps motive offers Debussy an opportunity to put it into another completely unexpected harmonic context. Just when we think we have heard every harmonization imaginable, Debussy discovers a new one. Each version is enriched by all of the others. Each one reveals some new emotion or expression hidden in these two simple footsteps.

Haydn Redux

To put this concept of compared-to-what in perspective, I want to return to our Haydn quartet for the final example of the chapter. We have already dealt extensively with Haydn's three different versions of his opening idea. But what about his second idea? (See example 35, measures 6 through 16.) When we first hear it, it seems to be as straightforward as the opening idea was confusing. A simple repeated-note accompaniment gets started and then continues underneath an equally simple tune played by the first violin and then by the cello. Things could not be more crystal clear. The accompaniment is utterly ordinary and without interest; the second violin and the viola do nothing but play the same notes over and over again. The catchy melody is clearly the focus, and repeating it in the cello firmly imprints it in the listener's ear. We "get" this idea.

Eight measures later it returns transposed lower.

EXAMPLE 39

This transposed repeat perfectly confirms and cements our understanding of this idea. Everything is copied exactly. The second violin and the viola play the same accompaniment figure (transposed), and the first violin and the cello play the same melody (transposed). All is still well with the world. (Remember from chapter 3, repetition clarifies meaning.) However, whenever something seems this straightforward in Haydn, you are almost invariably being set up, and this spectacular example is no exception.

Before the moment of compared-to-what revelation arrives, Haydn spends twelve measures developing the combo package from our opening idea at a breathtakingly fast pace. The speed of the musical thought is so quick that we have to struggle to keep up, so when the passage finally washes out on something we can understand and follow without effort—our simple repeated-note accompaniment figure—we breathe a sigh of relief.

EXAMPLE 40

[continued]

EXAMPLE 40 [continued]

   We know how this story goes. We have heard it twice before. The
accompaniment figure (transposed again) will "tick" seven times
(beginning on the downbeat) and then continue underneath our
melody. (Again, you don't think any of this consciously, it is simply
"the way the phrase goes." Having heard it twice, you internalize it
and expect it when it starts up a third time.) For seven blissful ticks
our expectations are confirmed, and then the world as we knew it
explodes. Though every fiber of our being expects the violin to come
in with its melody on the last note of measure 47, it doesn't. The two
lower parts simply continue their ticking, and then as if that isn't bad
enough, when the other parts finally do come in, they still don't play
the melody. Instead they join the ticking of the lower parts and turn
the repeated-note accompaniment figure (previously just a folklike,
hollow, two-part, open-fifth interval) into a four-part dissonant chord.
Our understanding of this idea has just been turned completely upside
down. We thought that this idea was "about" a catchy melody plus an
insignificant accompaniment. Now the "main attraction," the catchy
melody, has completely disappeared, and the insignificant accompaniment has become the star of the show. The key plot element!
   Passages like this, in which Haydn forces us to reevaluate our most
basic understanding of a musical idea, had an enormous influence on
Beethoven. The *Eroica* Symphony's theme-and-variations finale (see
chapter 8 for an extended discussion of theme and variations) starts
off as if it is going to be even more straightforward than our Haydn
example. After a brief introduction, Beethoven presents an almost
childishly simple, clear-cut theme and treats it to two absolutely text-

book variations. As with Haydn, we think we know how this story goes, and we are ready for several more delightful, decorative variations. But variation 3 forces a complete compared-to-what reevaluation. Suddenly, a brand-new melody emerges to become the "real" theme of the movement. In a bizarre plot twist worthy of Haydn, our simple, straightforward opening tune turns out not to be the movement's main theme at all but rather the bass line, or the accompaniment to the "real" main theme. And if this isn't shocking enough, the opening tune eventually disappears from the movement altogether. This is the plot of a master storyteller. A quintessential main theme becomes a bass line and then ultimately disappears.

Music like this can be a thrilling challenge to keep up with. Nothing is what it first appears to be; as is so often true in life, just when we think we understand what something means, circumstances and contexts change, and we are forced to reevaluate. Heraclites said, "No man ever steps in the same river twice, for it's not the same river and he's not the same man." Who we are is not who we were, nor who we will become. And so it is with a musical idea. The context, the stream, is always changing. Meaning must be pieced together by comparing each moment to what came before and what comes after as we follow the dynamic unfolding of each musical story through the magic of compared-to-what listening.

[6]

Forward–Backward
Listening

---

*Life can only be understood backwards . . . but it must be
lived forwards.*

—SØREN KIERKEGAARD

O ur discussion of compared-to-what listening has led us directly
to one of the most important concepts in this book; a concept
I call "forward-backward" listening. As we saw in chapter 5, the
meaning of a musical idea is almost never immediately apparent. Only
after a theme has been developed and heard in multiple contexts over
the course of an entire piece can we begin to grasp its sense. Musical meaning is constantly changing, and we piece together this meaning by comparing each moment to what came before and what
comes after. Consequently, there is an inevitable difference between
our understanding of a musical idea as we listen to it going forward
in time not knowing how it will turn out, and again once we have
heard how it ends. This difference is central to the dynamic experience of listening to music. Only when a phrase, a section, a movement, or an entire piece ends can we look back and understand what
it means. But how can you listen to music forward and backward at
the same time?

A Forward–Backward Nursery Rhyme

Because this concept is so crucial to understanding how musical narratives develop and resolve, I want to first give you a feel for how it works using a simple nursery rhyme, "Twinkle, Twinkle Little Star," as a forward-backward listening laboratory. For the sake of this elementary discussion, imagine you are hearing the song for the first time.

EXAMPLE 41

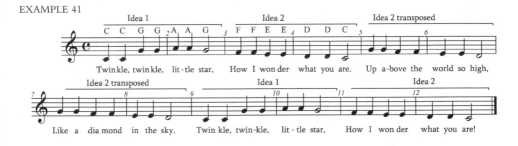

The song begins with two C's; one beat each, on "Twink-le." We then make a relatively large leap for a nursery rhyme to two G's; one beat each, for a second "twink-le." If you happen to be a highly attentive listener with an excellent ear, even on first hearing you might subliminally notice some relationship between the first and second "twinkles" without having time to pin it down. The song moves on.

"Little" moves up only a step, to two A's—one beat each—and we begin to sense a pattern. Every note is one beat long and is repeated twice. But then comes something new: "star" has only one note. It is not repeated, and it lasts for two beats, beautifully creating a slight pause, or comma, in the musical sentence. And this pause allows us a split second to *look backward* and group the entire seven notes into a unit; a tiny opening phrase in some longer musical sentence. This happens subconsciously in an instant, the way you grasp the rhythmic pattern of "Humpty Dumpty," for example, without even thinking about it. In "Twinkle, Twinkle Little Star," as in life, we are moving forward with little time to reflect, but we at least grasp *retrospectively* that the group of seven notes (three repeated-note pairs plus a single note) has become an idea, whereas the notes were isolated experiences going forward. Backward understanding is all about grouping experiences that were isolated when lived forward, and this new grouping or pattern sticks in our mind as we move to part 2.

Now things start to get interesting. "How I" (F–F) continues our repeated-note and rhythmic pattern, which we now begin to expect. As when learning the syntax of a foreign language (which each new piece of music is), we begin to grasp the idea that repeated one-beat notes are the piece's basic unit of grammar. When "won-der" (E–E) and "what you" (D–D) move down the scale in the same pattern, our entire body "expects" a single two-beat note to end this second thought, just like "star" ended the first, to make a kind of musical rhyme. And satisfyingly it does, with a single, two-beat C on "are." Depending on our musical ear, we may or may not realize consciously that we have come back to the note we started the song on—C. No matter. In any case we feel comforted, having completed a second unit with the same rhythm as the first while landing back on the note we started from. We can do the rest of the song quickly.

"Up a–bove the world so high" (G–G, F–F, E–E, D) is another unit of three repeated-note pairs plus a single note that moves down a scale in a familiar way. (Probably no clearer than that the first time through.) Then comes a gift for the listener: "Like a dia-mond in the sky" repeats the melody of "Up above the world so high" exactly. (Remember, we are not sure of this going forward until the last note—"sky.") Then we finish with a musical bookend, as the opening words and music repeat for "Twinkle, twinkle little star, / How I wonder what you are."

What Just Happened?

What basic facts do we now understand having come to the end of the first verse that we did not know going forward? Remember that grouping experiences is at the core of backward understanding. Going forward, we had no idea how long each musical phrase would be, and we had no idea how many phrases there would be in a verse. Now, looking backward, we know. Each tiny phrase contains seven notes, and six phrases make a verse. Knowing the size of the song's fundamental building blocks allows us to grasp its overall structure and rhythm, but it is not only the length of the phrases and the verse that we now understand looking backward; it is also the relationship *between* the phrases. Only when we have reached the last note do we understand retrospectively that all six tiny phrases have the identical structure. All six phrases are made up of three repeated-note pairs plus a single note. Bum-bum, bum-bum, bum-bum, BUM, six times! (Be sure to sing and check this in order to really internalize it.) That is why the song is so easy, reassuring, and satisfying for children to learn.

There is one more bit of backward understanding that is at the core of how this song works. Though the piece is six phrases long, it has only two melodic ideas. The first is the "Twinkle, twinkle little star" idea, the one with the leap (C–C, G–G, A–A, G). The second is the "How I wonder what you are" idea, the "four-notes-down-the-scale" idea (F–F, E–E, D–D, C). Everything else is either a repeat of one of these two ideas or a transposition. ("Up above the world so high / Like a diamond in the sky" is a transposition of the second idea, "four notes down the scale," which is followed by a repeat of the opening two phrases to bookend the stanza.) With only one rhythmic pattern and two melodic ideas, this is one of the most economical children's songs ever written.

What Does It Mean?

Though a greater appreciation of "Twinkle, Twinkle Little Star" is a minimally worthwhile goal, the important point here is not only to see clearly the difference between forward and backward listening in a simple piece of music, but to realize that this difference is at the heart of the listening experience. Because music exists in real time, listening to any piece, even one as simple as "Twinkle, Twinkle Little Star," involves a dynamic process of discovery as the meaning of the piece unfolds. All knowledge is provisional, and perpetually under revision. Each new measure changes the meaning of the measures that came before. We don't know as we hear the opening two phrases, "Twinkle, twinkle little star / How I wonder what you are," whether they will be important (i.e., heard from again). It is only when we hear the same two phrases return at the end of the stanza as a book-end that we in hindsight realize they are the song's refrain. And it is only after we have heard the entire song that we realize that they generate all of the musical material of the piece as well. As the song moves forward, we continually reevaluate the meaning of everything that came before, and it is not until the final note that we understand what the piece's musical materials mean.

Retrospective Music

This same fundamental forward-backward dynamic is at work in more complex music as well, and it operates on both the smallest and largest structural levels. As a tiny, small-scale example, take the opening phrase of Haydn's *Clock* Symphony.

EXAMPLE 42

After a mysterious, minor-key, slow introduction, the witty Presto begins with what seems to be a harmless, inconsequential "pickup" to the opening tune—an unaccompanied, slightly too long, seven-note scale in the first violins. (Pickups are generally one, two, or three notes.) The full string section enters in the next measure and begins what appears to be the real tune—a lively, regular, four-measure phrase. But then in a classic Haydnesque forward-backward surprise, the consequent phrase repeats not just the tune but the pickup scale as well. Just as with "Twinkle, Twinkle Little Star," these new measures completely change the meaning of the measures that came before. When we first hear the pickup scale, it doesn't occur to us that it might be important. It seemed to be nothing more than a little connector, an upbeat to the "real" tune. However, when the second half of the phrase includes a repeat of the pickup scale, we have to completely revise our understanding as we realize that this seemingly inconsequential scale is in fact an integral part of the tune. (A tune that we now realize *looking backward* is an irregular 5 + 5 measure phrase, not a regular 4 + 4 measure phrase.) And in case the repeat didn't make the scale's importance clear enough, the next measure turns the pickup scale into the main attraction, as the full orchestra bursts in, *forte*, with the pickup scale thickened to two parts while the lower strings and bassoon do the scale upside down. Just as with "Twinkle, Twinkle Little Star," as the piece moves forward we continually reevaluate the meaning of everything that came before, and were we to continue listening to the rest of the movement we would discover that the forward-backward reevaluations continue with surprise after surprise until the movement's final measure.

Forward-Backward Beethoven

Though the forward-backward reevaluations of Haydn's opening gesture in this short example are a vehicle for high comedy, the same principles in a different musical environment can structure an entire, highly dramatic movement. Let's look closely, in "Twinkle, Twinkle Little Star" fashion, at one rich Beethoven example.

EXAMPLE 43

The *Tempest* Sonata opens with a stunningly confusing, slow–fast, stop–and–start introduction. At first we have no idea what this first phrase could possibly mean. Beginning a piece of music with a slow introduction was not at all uncommon in the Classical period (in the same way that books often begin with a preface), and that is precisely what we assume is happening when we hear the opening slow arpeggio (a chord played one note at a time). But after only four slow notes, we suddenly get a burst of unrelated fast music. Is this fast music the "real" piece, the main body of the movement with a slow four-note introduction? For three fast measures we grope to understand, and then Beethoven stuns us (in measure 6) by lapsing back into the slow tempo.

This is an extraordinary forward–backward moment. We are back where we started in terms of tempo and key, yet even more confused than when we began. Beethoven opens the piece with what we thought was a slow introduction. Five seconds later he destroys that understanding and starts to work with fast music, as if the piece has really begun in earnest, and then he abruptly stops and retreats back to a slow tempo. So are we still in a slow introduction? Is this some new kind of slow introduction that is made up of slow *and* fast music? Beethoven marks a fermata in measure 6 over the last note of this phrase, and this fermata is all about forward–backward understanding. So many of Beethoven's most striking moments occur at fermatas when some note or chord is held at a point of maximum listener confusion. These pauses are designed to give the listener time to try and understand what has just occurred. To ask, "What is going on?" and most important, the key question when listening to Beethoven: "What is going to happen next?"

We have already seen in chapter 3 that repetition is one of the most fundamental ways composers create structural clarity in music. Anytime you repeat something, the listener begins to understand what it means, and as strange as this opening phrase is, if Beethoven had simply repeated it, we could have begun to grasp its sense. What Beethoven does instead is shocking: he repeats the opening slow arpeggio, but replaces the opening A-major arpeggio with a C-major arpeggio that is so totally unexpected it sounds like a mistake. As if the pianist had a memory slip and started to play in the wrong key. We are now completely lost. We don't know whether we are in an introduction or in the main body of the piece, we don't know whether the piece is fast or slow, and we don't have the faintest idea of what key it's in. And, of course, there is another fermata in measure 8 to prolong the agony. We truly have no idea what will come next. Fast music? Slow music? In what key?

Things rapidly go from bad to worse. Beethoven changes tempo again, transposes the original fast music for three notes, and then goes wild, stormily developing the fast section's ideas for twelve measures until the music finally arrives at a recognizable theme in measure 21. Though we clearly have arrived somewhere and the piece is now unmistakably under way, we still have no idea what the first twenty measures meant. Were they an introduction? Were they some strange kind of start-and-stop preface that we can now safely forget, that we'll never hear from again? We ask the same question we asked at measure 3: Is this new fast music we are currently hearing in measure 27 to measure 38 the "real" music of the piece, the main thematic material of the movement?

Are We There Yet?

In our short "Twinkle, Twinkle Little Star" and *Clock* Symphony examples, whatever we didn't understand about the piece going forward was resolved within seconds when we came to the end of a verse or a phrase and were able to look backward. Though we may not have understood the importance of Haydn's pickup scale when we first heard it, four measures later its repeat made its importance clear. Though we may not have understood the importance of the first two lines of "Twinkle, Twinkle Little Star" when we first heard them, within seconds, their importance as a refrain and a source of melodic material became clear. The time gap in these examples between confusion going forward and understanding looking backward is almost infinitesimal. However, the timescale of the *Tempest* Sonata is completely different. Not knowing what something means, or misunderstanding what something means for a considerable length of time, is an integral part of the listening experience with Beethoven's music. Making the listener wait, often for more than a hundred measures, before musical meaning is clarified is central to his aesthetic.

As we have already seen, when we reach measure 21 of the *Tempest* Sonata, we have no real idea what the first twenty measures were all about. But as more "regular" music with clear themes and continuous rhythm takes over, and as the piece starts to develop its own logic and momentum without any reference to the opening material (aside from the relationship of the opening arpeggio to the left-hand arpeggio theme of measures 21 and 22), our need to look back and understand the opening twenty measures begins to fade. As we get caught up in the dramatic music that follows, we are happy to leave the opening behind and provisionally understand it as some strange kind of introduction. We eagerly put its confusion behind us and move on.

Seventy-one measures later, however, the opening material returns. Though I will have much more to say about sonatas and the way they are put together in chapter 10, one of their conventions is to repeat the entire opening section of a movement, traditionally called the *exposition*. In the same way that on a smaller level repeating a motive or a phrase lets us know that the motive or phrase is a unit, repeating an entire exposition lets us know retrospectively that it is a unit. What was a continual surprise when heard the first time can be grasped as a whole the second time through. In the *Tempest* Sonata, the repeat of the exposition is shocking and transforms our most basic understanding of the piece. When we return to the opening to begin the repeat, we suddenly discover that this confusing, introductory, slow-fast, stop-start music that we had begun to forget is in fact part of the piece. It is not just a preface but rather material that must be integrated into the ongoing narrative of the sonata. And Beethoven makes no attempt to hide the effort this integration requires. All the dynamic energy and forward momentum the piece had developed by the end of the exposition must be willfully stopped, and we can feel the gears grind as Beethoven slows down the music in order to be able to return to the opening slow arpeggio.

EXAMPLE 44

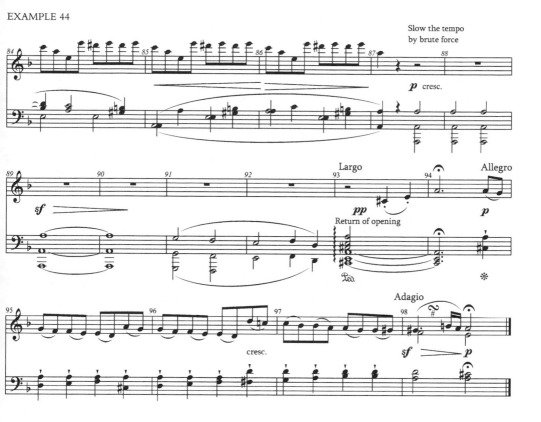

By repeating the entire opening, he forces us to accept this material as part of the ongoing narrative of the piece, but by no means completes our understanding of it. Were we to continue to look at the rest of the movement, we would hear this music come back at two key moments, each time forcing us to radically revise our understanding of the material yet again. These ongoing reevaluations, in which confusion becomes retrospective understanding again and again, are at the heart of what makes listening to music like this so dynamic and vital, but it is crucial to realize that both the confusion *and* the retrospective understanding are equally important.

How Things Turn Out

Let me put this in a slightly larger context. When we hear the first two lines of "Twinkle, Twinkle Little Star," we have no idea whether they are a structural key to the rest of the song—the germ of all that follows. How do we know they are important? Because they *turn out* to be both a bookend to the verse and the ultimate source of all of the piece's melodic material. How do we know that the opening of the *Tempest* Sonata is important? Because it *turns out* to be a part of the ongoing narrative of the piece as it proceeds, shaping key moments in the movement in significant ways. How things turn out plays a key role in shaping the way we understand earlier events, not only in music but in life as well. Though we are all aware of the enormous influence the past has on the future, we must never ignore the critical and ever-changing way the future—how things turn out—influences our understanding of the past. And we must also remember that how things turn out depends on when we choose to look back.

In the *Eroica* Symphony finale we discussed in chapter 5, a tune that begins as a quintessential main theme becomes an accompanying bass line two variations later, and eventually disappears. What the tune means depends on when we look back. At the end of variation 2, it is the "featured attraction": the main theme. By the end of variation 3, it has become less significant: an accompanying bass line to the new main theme. By variation 5 it has vanished altogether. Its meaning, like all musical meaning, is not static but dynamic. Backward understanding does not occur in a single moment. It is an ongoing, evolving, ever-changing process. Things are continually turning out in a piece of music, and each new development changes our retrospective understanding of everything that came before.

Walking in the Fog

In music as in life, our understanding of events as they occur is different from our understanding when we look back on them later. But it is crucial to realize that though it might be tempting to forget the messiness and confusion of the real-time, "lived-forward" version, in favor of the tidier, more rational, "understood-backward" version, neither version is privileged. A discussion of a piece of music that includes *only* the understanding gained after countless hours of retrospective analysis and dismisses the all-important initial listening experience the piece was largely designed for is a pointless academic exercise, just as any retrospective understanding of a personal experience that does not also include the chaos, confusion, exhilaration, and discovery of the lived moment is incomplete. *Both* forward and backward understandings are valid. Meaning is a process. We live forward and understand backward, perpetually reevaluating our experiences, and all of these understandings are true.

In *Testaments Betrayed*, the Czech author Milan Kundera reminds us that "man proceeds in the fog. But when he looks back to judge people of the past, he sees no fog on their path." The never-ending experience of confusion, giving way to understanding, giving way to new confusion and new understanding is at the heart of great listening. But whatever understanding we might reach looking back, we must never forget or diminish the importance of the confusing, lived-forward experience of fog. Kundera asks, "Who is more blind? . . . [the man walking in fog,] or we, who judge him decades later and do not see the fog that enveloped him?" Music, like life, is meant to be lived forward *and* understood backward.

[7]

The Challenge of Memory

The true art of memory is the art of attention.

—SAMUEL JOHNSON

We are now in a position to tackle head-on an important topic that has been lurking in the background of our discussion since chapter 1: the challenge of memory. As we have seen in previous chapters, the meaning of a musical idea is almost never immediately apparent. Every time an idea is developed, our understanding of it must be revised. Only after a theme has been heard in multiple contexts over the course of an entire piece can we begin to grasp its sense. Aaron Copland stated, "It is insufficient merely to hear music in terms of the separate moments at which it exists. You must be able to relate what you hear at any given moment to what has just happened before and what is about to come afterward." This is absolutely true, but in order to do this a listener must have one essential capacity—the ability to remember.

Remembering Callahan

I mentioned in chapter 1 that writers of film and television dramas assume that their audiences are capable of following and remembering plot developments throughout the course of a one-, two-, or even three-hour program. In the climactic scene at the end of the movie *Dirty Harry*, Inspector Callahan (played by Clint Eastwood) points his gun at the killer he has now cornered and wounded. As the killer lies sprawled on the ground with his gun only a foot out of reach, Callahan says:

> I know what you're thinking. "Did he fire six shots or only five?" Well, to tell you the truth, in all this excitement I kind of lost track myself. But being as this is a .44 Magnum, the most powerful handgun in the world, and would blow your head clean off, you've got to ask yourself a question: "Do I feel lucky?" Well, do ya, punk?

The killer decides that Callahan is bluffing and goes for his gun, and Callahan shoots him with his one remaining bullet. Though this is a classic action-movie moment, what really makes the scene great is that it is a variation on an almost identical encounter that occurred nearly an hour earlier in the film. In the earlier scene, Callahan delivers the same speech to another cornered criminal who backs down and surrenders, only to discover that Callahan was bluffing and had no bullets left. The final scene not only depends on the audience's remembering the general details of a scene that happened nearly an hour earlier, it depends on the audience's remembering Callahan's exact words. In fact, it depends on the audience's recognizing the speech from its opening two lines. By the time Callahan has said, "I know what you're thinking. 'Did he fire six shots or only five?'" the audience must flash back to the earlier scene, remember the dialogue and the outcome, and bring a detailed memory of the earlier scene with them as a context for the final encounter. And it works. You can almost hear the audience finishing Callahan's speech along with him. The screenwriter's assumptions about the identity of the audience and what they will or will not be able to remember could not be more on the mark.

Remembering Schumann

Composers' assumptions about their audience are just as explicit. Take the climactic moment of Robert Schumann's great Piano Quintet. The piece as a whole is approximately thirty minutes long and is divided into four substantial movements. The final movement is based on a catchy opening tune that returns several times in several different settings. After 247 measures and nearly a full movement's worth of compositional work, Schumann decides to turn this tune into the subject of a fugue. (More to come on fugue in general in chapter 9.)

EXAMPLE 45A

[continued]

EXAMPLE 45A [continued]

Schumann assumes that the listener will not only remember the main theme of the movement and recognize it when it becomes the subject of the fugue, but that he will also remember the theme's original context and appreciate how completely different it sounds in the almost academic fugal setting. This is actually not that difficult, as Schumann could not be more helpful. The "sticky" main theme is simple to remember, even on first hearing, due to its inner repetitions. The initial four-measure idea in example 45A actually repeats four times within the theme itself. In addition, the complete tune repeats several times throughout the movement, and in perhaps the most helpful touch of all, Schumann repeats it a final time in the section that immediately precedes the fugue to make the connection clear.

Things are not so simple for the listener, however, in the section that follows: the climactic moment not only of the movement, but of the entire piece. After the fugue on the fourth-movement theme finishes, the music gradually builds to an enormous climax and pauses with incredible anticipation on a fermata. After an electrifying silence (also marked with a fermata), the coda, or final section of the movement, begins a second fugue, using the main theme of the first movement as the subject, with each note stretched to twice its original length.

EXAMPLE 45B

Even granting that the first movement's main theme is a memorable one and is heard many times during the opening movement, Schumann is asking the listener not only to remember a theme that has not been heard in approximately twenty minutes, but also to recognize it stretched out to twice its original length as a fugue subject. This is a considerable challenge, but Schumann clearly believed his audience was up to it. Closing a piece with a fugue on its first- and last-movement themes is a quintessential tying-up-of-loose-ends, unifying gesture, and Schumann never would have written this kind of climactic connection if he thought it would go unnoticed.

Remembering X

Stating the challenge of memory in its simplest terms, to be able to compare two things—*x* and *y*—you must first be able to remember *x*. On many different levels and in many different ways, the ability to remember *x* has been an unstated core requirement throughout our entire discussion of plot, repetition, cadences, compared-to-what listening, and forward-backward understanding. To appreciate the witty way Haydn removes the pauses in the second version of his quartet opening (The End *pause*, The End *pause*) you must remember the first version (The End *pause-pause-pause*, The End *pause-pause-pause*). To appreciate the way Janáček compresses his original 8 + 9-note theme to 5 + 4 notes, you must remember the original version. To appreciate the warmth and color of Debussy's richly harmonized "footsteps," you must remember the austere grayness of the original version.

The faith that composers have put in their audiences' ability to remember is remarkable, and Franz Schubert's *Unfinished Symphony* is a beautiful and subtle example. The piece begins with an enigma (see example 46). When the cellos and the basses play their evocative opening—low in pitch, softly, in unison, without any harmony—we have absolutely no idea what is happening. As with the *Tempest* Sonata we wonder: Is this a slow introduction? Is it the actual opening theme? Because it's so low, perhaps it's actually a bass line, an accompaniment to the theme? Without any explanation, Schubert simply leaves the idea hanging and moves on to other material. With no answer forthcoming, we become involved in the music that follows, and the opening idea and its accompanying questions gradually fade from our consciousness.

EXAMPLE 46

For one hundred measures, we hear nothing more from this opening theme. Then in a subtle poetic stroke, it returns, transposed higher (starting on an E, not a B) to begin the development section. If Schubert had copied the original version, it would have gone like this.

EXAMPLE 47

But instead, he subtly changes the ending so that instead of leaping up and holding a final note as it did in the opening version, it continues downward, one amazing note at a time, descending into uncharted depths (below the range of a normal double bass, requiring an extension to play the lowest notes) to discover a new kind of expression in a mysterious low register. The lengthy development section that follows is almost exclusively based on highly imaginative transformations of this long-absent opening idea. For one hundred measures, Schubert expects the listener to remember *x*—an almost inaudible theme, played once, *pianissimo*, in the lowest regions of the cellos and basses—and for more than 150 years listeners have risen to the challenge.

Remembering *X*, *Y*, and *Z*

Though Schubert's *Unfinished Symphony* asks the listener to remember a single theme, heard once, for a hundred measures, many pieces pose even greater memory challenges. Music in which ideas are continually developed and return multiple times in different contexts not only assumes a listener capable of remembering *x*, but a listener capable of remembering *x*, *y*, and *z*. To see how this works, let's return one last time to our Haydn quartet and look at how the opening idea finally resolves itself. We have already seen that to appreciate the witty way Haydn removes the pauses in his second version you must remember the first version. Though the lengths of the pauses in the two versions are different, both versions are made up of two statements of "The End plus silence," followed by the "combo package." The climactic moment occurs when this opening theme returns to begin the recapitulation. (For more on recapitulation, see chapter 10.) As we will see in our later discussion of the sonata, recapitulations do not simply repeat earlier material, they resolve compositional problems. They tell us what is important, and we expect to finally find out which version, x or y, is the "real" version: the version Haydn will bring back. Haydn absolutely assumes that we not only noticed the difference between the two versions when we heard them at the opening of the movement, but that we remember and are breathlessly waiting to see which one will return. Here is Haydn's "resolution."

EXAMPLE 48

If you are listening in compared-to-what, forward-backward fashion, these four measures are fantastic, and they are as close to quintessential Haydn as can be imagined. Rather than choosing either x or y as the "real" theme, Haydn chooses z: a third version! First let's look at the melody. Though both earlier versions were made up of two statements of The End plus silence, followed by the combo package, this version wittily adds an extra third statement before the combo package. Not The End *pause*, The End *pause* plus the combo package, but The End *pause*, The End *pause*, The End **pause** plus the combo package. And if that's not enough, the second violin dazzlingly fills in the rests with a brand-new, brilliant, high-speed scale figure invented just for this moment. Though this climactic version whizzes by in approximately five seconds and refers back to two versions that were heard 173 measures earlier, Haydn clearly believed his audience would remember x and y, compare them to z, and be delighted.

Rejecting Memory

Before we put this discussion in context, it is impossible not to look at what is probably the most famous example of musical memory in all of classical music: the finale of Beethoven's Ninth Symphony. Though the ability to remember is an implicit requirement for listening to all of the music we have been discussing, the Ninth Symphony makes the *rejection* of memory an explicit component of its musical content.

EXAMPLE 49

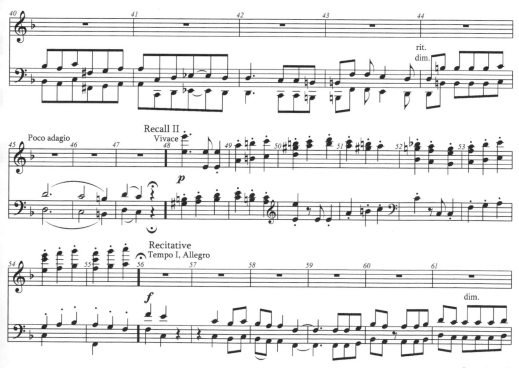

[continued]

EXAMPLE 49 [continued]

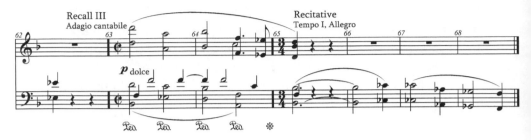

Today we have grown accustomed to the gigantic symphonies of
Anton Bruckner and Gustav Mahler, and we tend to forget how radical the sheer scope of Beethoven's symphonies was in his day. Nearly
every contemporary review of the *Eroica* Symphony commented on
its unprecedented length, and the Ninth Symphony, with a running
time of an hour or more (twice as long as Schumann's Piano Quintet),
was even longer. Beethoven's music was not only longer than the
music of his contemporaries, but it also made demands on the long-
range hearing of his listeners that went far beyond those of any previous composer. The Ninth Symphony finale comes after three full
movements of enormously complex music have already gone by. The
finale begins with a dissonant, tumultuous, lurching scream, played by
woodwinds, brass, and timpani and broken off by the double basses,
which in a passage of instrumental recitative (speechlike instrumental music), reject this opening. A second assault, higher and more
intense, is again rejected by the basses. Unable to move forward, on
the verge of collapse, Beethoven searches through past modes of
expression for a language in which to continue. He first quotes the
opening eight measures of the first movement. Though at least forty
minutes have gone by since we heard this passage, Beethoven assumes
not only that the first-time listener will instantly remember it, but also
that he will do so, as moviegoers will with Inspector Callahan's speech,
from hearing only two short phrases. To be precise, slightly less than
two short phrases, as the double basses interrupt before the second
phrase has even finished.

After the basses have rejected this memory with another passage of
instrumental recitative, Beethoven brings back eight measures of the
quick-tempo second movement. Though this brief recall lasts no
more than five seconds, Beethoven clearly believes it contains enough

material from the earlier movement for the listener to recognize it some fifteen minutes after its first appearance. And it works. The basses interrupt this memory as well, and the third-movement recall that follows is the most concentrated of all, quoting nothing but the movement's first six melody notes. Beethoven's attitude toward memory is clearly expressed by all of the bass and cello recitatives, which reject these recalls and essentially declare in instrumental fashion what the solo baritone singer will later put literally into words: "O friends, not these sounds; but let us rather sing more pleasant and joyful ones." In the finale, the past is called into recollection in order to be rejected. "Not these sounds," Beethoven says, but new ones, "more joyful ones," must be found if we are to move forward. Yet even Beethoven's explicit rejection of memory is accomplished by remembering x. To reject the past, we must first remember it.

Cultural Memory

It is interesting that today we live in a culture that places an enormously high value on history, but almost no value on memory. It is hard to imagine a time period in which researching, studying, and writing about the past have ever enjoyed more widespread cultural support, yet at the same time the faculty of memory has rarely seemed less important. Memorization of any kind, particularly when attached to its seemingly ubiquitous companion word, *rote*, is now routinely viewed as the antithesis of "real" education. Memorizing poetry, once a staple of classroom learning, is now seen to be as antiquated and old-fashioned as studying Latin. Teachers apologize for asking students to memorize anything—facts, dates, poems, tables, verb endings, or scientific formulas—and foreign-language tapes advertise, "Learn a foreign language . . . without memorization!" Though this might seem to be a purely modern phenomenon, more than two thousand years ago Socrates feared that the loss of memory would be an inevitable by-product of the discovery of the "brand-new" phonetic alphabet. According to Plato's *Phaedrus*, Socrates worried that:

> This discovery will create forgetfulness in the learners' souls, because they will not use their memories; they will trust to the external written characters and not remember of themselves.

> The [alphabet] which you have discovered is an aid not to memory but to recollection, and gives only a semblance of truth; they will hear much and learn nothing; they will appear to know much and will generally know nothing; they will be tiresome company, for they will seem wise without being wise.

It is fascinating that Socrates' belief was echoed by Native Americans more than a thousand years later, when they made contact with white men for the first time. The tribes that met the settlers were astonished by their need to write things down and assumed this could only be a reflection of the White Man's inferiority and weak memory. In fact, the Shoshone word for "white people" means "those who write things down." Like the Greeks, the Indians prided themselves on the memory required to sustain their oral cultures, and since there was no need to transmit this knowledge outside of the tribe, there was no need for writing. For Socrates, like Native Americans, real engagement came through memory, not through the written word. When you memorized something, you internalized it, took possession of it, made it your own, made it live inside of you. Writing it down kept it separate and removed. Outside of you. Today, however, we seem to believe the opposite. We think of memorization as a mechanical, distancing activity producing no real engagement with the memorized material, simply the ability to "parrot" it back.

But if this is true, how do we explain the role of memory in the world of pop music? Even in Top 40 music, where the musical ideas and forms are generally short and repetitive (more on this in the next chapter), radio stations, realizing the crucial importance of memory, play current hits over and over again, hour after hour, until listeners know every nuance of the new songs by heart. A song doesn't really arrive on the popular landscape until teens everywhere can sing along with it from beginning to end. Memorizing popular songs (watch fans mouthing every word at a rock concert) is the way listeners make the music their own. It is the way they take something outside of themselves and move it inside.

Interestingly enough, something similar goes on for anyone who performs a piece of music from memory. Though it is of course completely possible to enter a composer's mind-set while playing from printed music, there is something special about internalizing and owning music so that you can play it by memory, without the need for external reminders. As it does for the teenage listener who memorizes a pop song, memorizing a composer's music brings you into someone else's world and makes it your own. When you perform a piece of music "by heart" (the unusual phrase itself suggests the intimacy of the connection), you create the illusion that it is your own piece, your own expression, your own story. In fact, the strange classical-music conventions that have grown up surrounding performing by memory in public (regarding who does or doesn't have to do it) seem to reflect this storytelling source. It is the performers in musical forms that come closest to dramatic narrative—opera singers, vocal soloists, concerto soloists, and solo pianists, who are "required" to perform by memory in order to create the illusion that the story they are telling is their own.

As Socrates suggests, for both the listener and the performer, the process of memorization creates intense engagement with the thing being remembered. In the music we have been discussing, composers use memory as a tool to construct the shared context of a piece together with a listener. Remembering, comparing, and reevaluating as a piece of music proceeds is the way a listener participates in its process, and this activity not only allows him to enter the composer's world, but to co-create it. People often talk about the enormous task of teaching people to understand music, when what is really required is to get them to hear it fully. It is not more musical knowledge that is needed, but rather the ability to listen completely. To pay attention, notice, and *remember*. As Ralph Waldo Emerson said, "It is the good reader that makes the good book," and good listening begins with remembering.

[8]

Form Is a Verb

―――――――

Line by line and passage by passage the poem comes to the poet from sources he feels strongly but does not pretend to understand. At least at the beginning of the poem. Very soon however, whatever comes to him from the je-ne-sais-quoi had better start coming in response to what he has already written down or he is not going to have a poem. Maybe the first line comes from nowhere. And maybe the second comes from a second-theme nowhere. But whatever part of what follows continues to come to him from his nowhere, it has to come from those first lines as well. The poem, that is, is forever generating its own context. Like a piece of music, it exists as a self-entering, self-generating, self-complicating, self-resolving form.

—JOHN CIARDI, *HOW DOES A POEM MEAN?*

Having worked our way from idea, to phrase, to section, in the next several chapters we will apply what we have learned to a discussion of the listening principles at the heart of some of classical music's most fundamental forms. In considering these forms, I am not interested in musical taxonomy—laying out and labeling each "species" of form with an accompanying schematic diagram—but rather in getting at the different kinds of musical logic these forms contain and the different kinds of listening they require. Learning to define a form is much less important than learning how to experience it. How does the experience of listening to a fugue differ from the experience of listening to a sonata or a minuet? What do composers want us to hear? To use Ciardi's language, how do these different forms "mean"?

The concept of form is not only at the core of musical meaning, but it is also an intrinsic part of the very definition of composition. The dictionary defines *compose* as "To put together, put in proper order or form." The word itself comes from joining *com* (with) and *poser* (to place): "to place with." Exploring the different ways musical ideas are "placed with" other musical ideas so that they create "proper order or form" will be the focus of these chapters. To quickly establish some basic listening principles, I want to first look outside the world of classical music at one of the clearest and most ubiquitous forms in all of popular music: the thirty-two-bar song form.

It is an article of faith in almost every critical discussion of artistic form that form and content are inseparable. Form, the argument goes, is not simply an existing mold into which new content is poured, but rather something that is shaped in each case by the particular details of the work in question. Because the content of every piece is unique, all forms are, in a sense unique, and the listener's job is to hear how each particular form grows out of its particular content. Though all of this is absolutely true, it slightly oversimplifies the situation. Every sonata of Haydn's *is* unique, and it *is* almost impossible to find one that fits any textbook definition of sonata form, while the enormous variety of formal structures in the fugues of Bach has led critics to stop even referring to fugue as a form, calling it instead "a way of writing." However, though it may be true, for example, that what is valuable about any particular haiku is the unique way its individual thought is expressed—if in three unrhymed lines of five, seven, and five syllables—it is actually the complex interplay between what is fixed and what is free that is interesting: the way each individual haiku finds its own unique shape within a seemingly rigid, external mold. And the process by which each haiku constructs its particular seventeen-syllable shape, word by word, is its form. Form is happening at every moment, as every word is chosen. Form is an action. Form is a verb.

Popular Music

Perhaps the closest musical parallel to the haiku's rigid form and clearly defined interplay between what is fixed and what is free is the form at the heart of the Broadway musical: the thirty-two-bar song form. The overwhelming dominance of this form in the repertoire of the musical is astonishing. Though no one I know of has ever done any statistical computations, I would venture to guess that the thirty-two-bar song form provides the structure, with slight variations, of nearly 90 percent of all theater songs. It is as standardized as a haiku or a sonnet, and along with the twelve-bar blues, it is one of America's most enduring musical forms. It is also an amazingly courageous and self-confident one. In the standard version, twenty-four of the thirty-two measures consist of the same music. That in and of itself is an extraordinary fact. Seventy-five percent of the music consists of a single eight-measure melody repeated three times. In a conventional Broadway song, beginnings literally are everything. Let's walk through the form and see how it works.

"I Got Rhythm" Redux

Since the opening idea is the key to the entire song, the form invariably starts with a catchy idea, eight measures in length, like the opening of "I Got Rhythm," which we looked at in chapter 2. Call the opening idea A.

EXAMPLE 50

[continued]

EXAMPLE 50 [continued]

[continued]

EXAMPLE 50 [continued]

The form then repeats the music of A with different words ("I got daisies, / In green pastures, / I got my man, / Who could ask for anything more?"), followed by a contrasting section of eight bars, call it B. ("Old Man Trouble, / I don't mind him, / You won't find him, / 'Round my door.") The standard form finishes by repeating the opening A music a third time, yet again with new words. ("I got starlight, / I got sweet dreams, / I got my man, / Who could ask for anything more?") In a slight variation on the form, "I Got Rhythm" adds an extra two measures to finish the song by wittily repeating the words "Who could ask for anything more?" The complete standard thirty-two-bar form is: A (eight measures), A (eight measures), B (eight measures), A (eight measures).

Let's look closely at some key listening principles embedded in this clear, simple form. The poet John Ciardi said,

> A poem may well be conceived as a machine for making choices. At any given point in the poem, the poet must select

the next thing to do. He must choose a word, an idea, an image—all these together. He must choose from the total language one word and not another.

Though the image of a machine perhaps conveys a more mechanical, automatic, deterministic quality than is appropriate, the idea is directly applicable to musical form. A musical form is also a "machine for making choices" and a standardized, highly structured form like the thirty-two-bar song form is a "machine" that influences (without determining) every musical choice, from first note to last. As in a haiku, there is a subtle interplay between what is fixed and what is free. Though each theater song shapes its particular content to meet the form's structural requirements in its own unique way, simply knowing that your opening idea must be exactly eight measures long—not four, six, or ten—acts like a filter to exclude an enormous number of musical possibilities. It tends to lead to songs (like haikus) with short, striking ideas rather than ideas that develop gradually over time. Unlike the openings we looked at in chapter 2, popular-song openings like the Gershwins', do not ask the listener to wait. They instantly create character and atmosphere and unfold their musical stories within clear, self-contained, eight-measure units. Like haiku, the thirty-two-bar song form is not for novelists or essayists, but for aphorists: musical quick-sketch artists like the Gershwins.

Let's use "I Got Rhythm" as a way of getting at the listening principles built into this form. We have already seen in chapter 2 how the syncopated rhythm that opens the song immediately hooks the listener and is then repeated just enough times to become a pattern, set up an expectation, and prepare us for the surprise punch line ("Who could ask for anything more?"). We also saw how the melody's four simple pitches (C, D, F, and G) played forward, backward, and then forward again, make the punch line's new melody surprising and witty as well. Since all form is ultimately about how phrases are "placed with" other phrases, it is always important to listen closely at cadence points to hear how phrases connect—how seams are made. Notice the elegant way that the ending of the tune leads back to the beginning with three jazzy "turnaround" beats at the end of measure 8. (The term *turnaround* refers to the way the chords "turn around" the end of the phrase so it can repeat itself.) Remember this ending when we come to the final phrase of the song.

After the A section, the Gershwins repeat the music with new words. Repeating something is always a key form-defining moment, and repetition is at the heart of nearly all large-scale form. As we will see in later chapters, the element that is repeated may be different in different forms (e.g., a phrase, a fugue subject, a bass line, a harmonic pattern, a theme group, a rondo tune, an exposition, etc.), but some repeated element is a core organizing principle in nearly all forms. Here, repeating A lets us know that A is a unit. Repetition allows the listener to retrospectively group the opening eight measures into a single idea.

"Home"–"Away"–"Home"

What happens next exhibits another fundamental principle of form: contrast. Since three of the four phrases in a thirty-two-bar song form repeat the same music, the only contrast in the entire form is its eight-measure B section. In the Gershwins' B section, not only is the melody completely new (though it does keep the A section's syncopated rhythm), but the harmony is as well. The chords are completely different from those in the A section. They're dynamic, unstable, and restless. The fundamental purpose of this B section is summed up by its letter designation: it is "not A." To be "not A" is a fundamental principle of form. Contrast on one level provides welcome, Stravinsky-like "variety" to balance the song's overwhelming "unity," but more important, B allows A to seem new and fresh when it returns. Leaving A—"home," the song's core tune—generates the desire to hear it again. This movement of "home–away–home" is basic to a wide range of forms. It is, for example, the essential principal behind all rondos. Though a rondo by Beethoven, Brahms, or Antonín Dvořák might have a "home" theme that is longer and more complex than that of "I Got Rhythm," and might move "away" to elaborate B, C, and D sections with transitions and developments to provide contrast, on the most fundamental level, "I Got Rhythm" and the rondo share the same core aesthetic. Put simply, rondos, like thirty-two-bar Broadway songs, are "about" their opening tunes. When we are "home" listening to that tune, we are structurally content. When we move "away" and leave the tune, as interesting and exciting as the contrasting sections (called *episodes* in a rondo) might be, on the most fundamental level we are always waiting to return "home," to the rondo tune. The longer we wait, the more intense the desire to return, and playing with listener impatience is the source of all of the witty passages of preparation in rondos (called *retransitions*) that delay this key moment. Leaving generates the desire to return in "I Got Rhythm" as it does in any classical or contemporary rondo, but it creates a problem for the Gershwins and every other Broadway songwriter when they try to end their songs.

Cadences Are Everything

As I mentioned earlier in the chapter, since all form is about how phrases are "placed with" other phrases, it is always important to listen closely at cadence points to hear how phrases connect—how seams are made. In the thirty-two-bar song form's AABA structure, the ending of A must perform three very different functions. The first time through, it must lead seamlessly back to the beginning of the tune. The second time through, it has to lead to the B section, while the third time through, it has to conclude the entire song. Remembering our discussion of the different degrees of finality of various cadences, in a thirty-two-bar song form, the same cadence must be a comma, a semicolon, and a period. In order to solve this formal problem, composers have come up with a remarkable variety of solutions. Some composers, like Irving Berlin with "Cheek to Cheek," repeat the melody absolutely identically all three times and simply alter the accompaniment underneath to create the punctuation the moment demands.

EXAMPLE 51A

EXAMPLE 51B

EXAMPLE 51C

Some composers, like Richard Rodgers with "I Wish I Were in Love Again," subtly alter the melody at each of the three endings, and the three different vocal cadences beautifully shape the structure of the entire song.

EXAMPLE 52A

EXAMPLE 52B

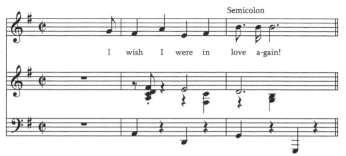

EXAMPLE 52C

The Gershwins, like Berlin, use the same vocal ending to return to the opening as well as to lead to the B section, while simply altering the accompaniment underneath to make the two different seams. However, the brilliant solution for the ending is all the Gershwins'. In the last A section, they alter the melody for "Who could ask for anything more?" so that it ascends this time, and they put a questioning harmony underneath. (A deceptive cadence to delay the final cadence and make it more conclusive.) They then add two extra measures to the form (eight, eight, eight, ten) to emphatically resolve the whole piece by repeating the words "Who could ask for anything more?" with the original vocal ending. A surprising yet utterly perfect conclusion.

Ex-Post-Facto Forms

One of the main reasons I have begun our discussion of form with the thirty-two-bar song form is because it is so clear and well defined, and one of the reasons it is so clear and well-defined is because composers were consciously aware that they were using it. Like someone writing a haiku today, the Gershwins, Berlin, and Rodgers knew the structure of the form before they began composing. Most musical forms, however, were "defined" after the fact by theorists looking back and generalizing from earlier practices. As we will see in chapter 11, the three greatest composers of Classical-period sonatas—Haydn, Mozart, and Beethoven—had no idea they were writing in sonata form. The textbook descriptions we know today were created by nineteenth-century theorists looking back on these masterpieces and were intended to be guides to composers for the production of future sonatas. Though these textbook forms are often highly inappropriate as descriptions of Haydn's, Mozart's, and Beethoven's sonatas, they are almost perfect guides to sonatas written *after* the Classical period, when composers began to follow these ex-post-facto descriptions. (Charles Rosen's two books, *The Classical Style* and *Sonata Forms*, contain insightful, comprehensive discussions of nineteenth-century descriptions of sonata form.)

Detailed forms with specific, spelled-out structural requirements, like the thirty-two-bar song form, are rare in music history. Baroque composers did not consult a textbook for the structural plan of a chaconne, a passacaglia, or a fugue before they wrote one any more than Beethoven looked up the plan for a sonata. What they did was look at other composers' music, and what they discovered there were not strict forms with fixed rules but storytelling patterns and procedures that arose naturally. These patterns were then imitated, varied, and developed from composer to composer and from piece to piece as the material demanded. When similar musical situations arise over and over again, it is not surprising that recurring plot solutions and variations on these solutions tend to evolve over time, and invariably theorists have come along to generalize from these similar solutions and turn them into abstract forms. Yet though two pieces of music might share similar or even identical external forms, it is the measure-by-measure way each piece traces that form that counts. Saying that two theater songs both begin with eight-bar A sections is a starting point for discussing their content but nothing more. *Form* here is not a noun—the diagram of a shape (AABA)—but a verb: the experience of tracing that shape. To make this crucial point in the clearest way possible, I would like to look briefly at an absolutely perfect, thirty-two-bar song form piece written approximately a hundred years before the term was even invented: Schumann's famous "Träumerei" ("Dreaming") from *Kinderszenen*.

EXAMPLE 53

[continued]

EXAMPLE 53 [continued]

"Träumerei"

Although there are enough wonderful details in this piece to fill an entire chapter, I want to focus solely on the ones that show the enormous range of musical possibilities offered by a single form. First let's make sure the overall form is clear. In "Träumerei," measures 1 through 8 are the opening, eight-bar A section of the piece. The double dots at the end of measure 8 are a sign to repeat the whole opening, and this repeat makes up the second eight-bar A section. Measures 9 through 16 are the contrasting, eight-bar B section, and measures 17 through 24 make up the final, eight-measure A section. "Träumerei" is an absolutely perfect thirty-two-bar song form: A (eight measures), A (eight measures), B (eight measures), A (eight measures).

The differences between Schumann's and the Gershwins' approaches to the form begin with the opening phrase and reflect two very different concepts of what constitutes a musical idea. The first four notes of "I Got Rhythm" immediately give us both the signature syncopated rhythm that dominates the entire song, and the four-note melodic idea that generates all but the punch line of the opening melody. Nothing about the Gershwins' opening asks the listener to wait for even a second. In "Träumerei," however, though the meaning of Schumann's opening idea dominates his entire composition as well, it will take the whole piece for that meaning to unfold.

Since this idea is the key to the song, let's look closely at its subtle construction. Rhythm is as central to this idea as it is to the Gershwins' but in a completely different way. Schumann's opening starts with three and a half beats of "settling in" music as the melody (the upbeat and downbeat are indicated by "And-1" on the music) waits for the chord underneath to fully come into play. The melody then rises in a graceful five-note arpeggio to an F (remember this F for later) and repeats the note with a beautiful held chord underneath to finish the idea. (Note the lovely quick grace notes in the left hand to emphasize the arrival.) If the Gershwins' opening rhythm "has rhythm," Schumann's subtle rhythm "dreams." A normal version of Schumann's opening would shorten the "settling in" process by one beat so that the long second chord could arrive on a downbeat, like this.

EXAMPLE 54

But Schumann's second melody note "dreams" for an extra beat, which causes the second chord to arrive poetically on a weak beat in the middle of measure 2. Once Schumann reaches his high F, the rest of the idea gradually winds its way back down to complete this phrase in measure 4 and begin a consequent phrase in measure 5.

Berlin's, Rodgers's, and the Gershwins' opening eight-measure phrases were all constructed in classic musical-comedy, unidirectional fashion to lead to "punch lines" in their final measures: "Who could ask for anything more?" (Gershwins), "When we're out together dancing cheek to cheek" (Berlin), and "I wish I were in love again" (Rodgers). Schumann's opening has a completely different kind of construction. It is a classically balanced, four-measures-plus-four-measures, antecedent-consequent phrase, and the entire consequent phrase is a beautiful variant of the antecedent. Measure 5 begins by repeating the "settling in" gesture of measure 1 (And–1) and then starts to repeat the graceful five-note arpeggio. But this time, in a classic compared-to-what moment, the music exquisitely arches up higher, to an A instead of an F, while the striking "dissonant" chord underneath the A has the first accidental (note outside the key) in the piece. Because the arpeggio this second time has risen higher, the route back down is different, and the details repay careful listening.

Having finished the first eight-bar A section, like the Gershwins, Schumann repeats it, but the purpose of Schumann's repeat is completely different from the Gershwins'. In a popular song, everything is dependent on the opening idea. As Richard Rodgers said, "If the song is successful, it's the idea that you walk out whistling." On the most basic level, in a theater song, all of the repetitions of the opening idea, not only within the song itself but in the overture, entr'acte, scene-change, and incidental music are designed to imprint it in every listener's ear. Schumann, however, is not repeating the opening eight measures so that the listener can whistle them, but so that he can retrospectively group the measures into a single unit and remember that unit as something to be developed and varied as the piece moves forward.

"Away"–"Home"

We saw that the Gershwins' eight-measure B section functions primarily as contrast, a move "away" from A so as to generate a desire to hear it again. The melody in the Gershwins' B section is new, though it keeps the A section's catchy signature rhythm, while the harmony is more restless. Schumann's B section (beginning in measure 9) also provides contrast, and has more restless harmony, but that is only the beginning of its story. It starts with the "settling in" music and the graceful ascending arpeggio, as if to start a third repeat of A. We have already heard this arpeggio ascend to an F and to an A, and the repeat has cemented these two versions in our ear. The B section now introduces yet a *third* version, which this time ascends to an E-flat in measure 10. (As always, the sound is what's important. Think of the letter names as labels.) Then, once we have gotten this third version in our ear, he transposes it in measure 13, using it to make the second half of the B section. At the same time, Schumann is not just quickly whisking through some restless chord changes like the Gersh-wins do in their B section but actually changing keys twice; first to G minor in measure 12, then to B-flat major in measure 13. And then, just on the verge of arriving in yet a third key (D minor in measure 16) at the last instant, with a ritardando (an indication to slow down) marked so the listener will not miss the moment, he shifts direction and magically arrives back "home" in F major to begin the final A section.

By now the listener has already had to process an enormous amount of sophisticated musical information in a short space of time, but Schumann has saved the best for last. Measure 17 begins the return of A, and the entire antecedent phrase is repeated exactly in measures 17 through 20. The whole climax of the piece, however, turns on an unbelievably subtle yet exquisite reharmonization. We come to our graceful ascending arpeggio for the final time. We have already heard four different versions. The melody now floats up to an A exactly as it did in measure 6, but Schumann completely changes the harmony underneath, discovering a miraculous, otherworldly chord somewhere in dreamland that transforms the color of this A. (Schumann writes a fermata to make sure we luxuriate in this incredible chord.) And then, as if that were not enough, he rewrites the final descent back home from this climax, with a last cadence that, like the Gershwins', sounds utterly right, but is truly surprising.

My purpose in looking at these two very different treatments of the same rigidly defined form was the hope that it would serve as a kind of cautionary example before we begin to explore other forms in upcoming chapters. In the end, all listening is particular. Though a form like the thirty-two-bar song form may exist as an abstract scheme in a textbook, what counts is the way it is lived piece by piece. Schumann's complex developmental approach to this thirty-two-bar form offers a completely different (not better or worse) kind of lis-tening experience than "I Got Rhythm." Yet both pieces are shaped, in very different ways, by their 8-8-8-8, AABA formal structure. In the end, what is important is the listener's ability to enter into the world of each piece and hear how its contents shape its particular form. A form may be a "machine for making choices," but the machine is wielded by human hands in unique ways. Measure by measure, phrase by phrase. Form is happening at every moment, as every note is chosen. Form is an action. Form is a verb.

[9]

From Dancing to Listening
Minuets and Scherzos

When the music changes so does the dance.

—AFRICAN PROVERB

Before moving forward in our discussion of form, I want to clear up a general point that has sometimes proved to be a source of confusion not only to newcomers to classical music but also to experienced listeners. The title of a piece does not necessarily tell you what form it is written in, nor does the name of a form tell you where it will be found. Though several of the forms we will be discussing in this and the following four chapters are traditionally associated with a particular genre of music, they frequently appear in other kinds of pieces as well, as the form of either complete movements or portions of movements. Fugues, for example, are a genre of music in and of themselves, but entire fugal movements or portions of movements, like the one we discussed in Schumann's Piano Quintet, can be found as part of sonatas, symphonies, quartets, masses, and other vocal works. Similarly, *sonata* is the name of both a form and a genre. Movements written in sonata form occur not only in pieces called sonatas but in nearly every other genre of Classical-period music. On the other hand, the individual movements of a three- or four-movement sonata for piano or violin are usually written in a variety of forms, including rondo form, aria form, or theme-and-variations form as well as sonata form. It is best to think of a form as a way of writing that can be used in many different genres and that can be adapted to many different musical contexts. The form we will be focusing on in this chapter is probably most often associated today with minuets and scherzos, but it has a long musical history and can be found in Baroque bourrées, hornpipes, and loures, as well as Classical-period theme-and-variation movements, and even twentieth-century dance suites by Bartók and Schoenberg. As with all of the forms we will be discussing, what I am interested in is the listening principles behind the form and the way it is shaped by the unique content of each particular piece. Because of this, I will refer to this chapter's form not by a genre-specific name like "minuet form" but by a more genre-free title: "two-repeat form."

From Life to Art

Because classical music today has largely become something we listen to in concert or on recordings, it is easy to forget the essential role it once played as a part of daily life. An enormous amount of the music written in the Baroque period and earlier was designed to support either the liturgical rituals of the church or secular activities at court, which frequently focused on dancing. Supplying music for dancing was an essential task for nearly every composer until the twentieth century, when popular music took over the job. Vast quantities of dance music—hornpipes, allemandes, bourrées, minuets, rigaudons, forlanes, and the like—were written in the Baroque period because people danced all the time, and composers had to supply music to match the demand. As time passed, however, dance music gradually became more abstract and sophisticated—"artified" so to speak—and eventually left its original real-world function behind. Put simply, the minuet, which was originally designed to be danced to, ultimately became something to listen to, and as with jazz, which also went from being "dance-to" music to "listen-to" music, the switch transformed both content and form.

Two-Repeat Form

A "Dance-to" Minuet

To get a sense of what the minuet was like when its function was purely to accompany dancing, here is a popular minuet from the early 1700s quoted in John Playford's famous eighteenth-century dance manual, *The Dancing Master*.

EXAMPLE 55

Everything about this minuet is connected to its function as an accompaniment to dance. What are the essential requirements for a piece of popular dance music? First and foremost, it must be danceable. This means that every aspect of the music's form must be clear and articulated. The dancers must always know where they are, and they must be able to follow not only the measure-by-measure rhythm of the music—which means it must have a steady, regular beat without confusing changes of pattern or accent—but the overall structure of the dance as well. If the choreography, for example, has sixteen moves with a shift of direction at the halfway point, the dancers must be able to know without thinking when the music has reached that point. If the dance closes with a distinctive physical gesture, the dancers must know when the music is about to end. The key feature that lets dancers know where they are in a minuet is repetition: the repetition of each half of the piece, indicated by the repeat signs marked at the end of each section. Though this might seem self-evident, the single most important aesthetic fact about the listening experience in all two-repeat pieces is that there are two repeats. Whatever the musical content, the listener hears both sections twice. Regularity and symmetry are built into the form. Even if the individual sections are completely irregular, when multiplied by two (heard twice) they become regular. A two-repeat form is also the quintessence of forward-backward listening. The first time through each section we hear the music unfold without knowing how it will turn out, while the second time through, having grasped the music of the section as a single unit, we follow its plot, understanding what it means.

"Dance-to" plots like the Playford minuet are different from "listen-to" plots. The Playford minuet opens with a catchy rhythm in its first measure—it is important for a piece of dance music to make dancers want to dance—but the idea is essentially abandoned and left undeveloped. Music that develops ideas in an ongoing way assumes a compared-to-what listener who is paying attention to musical detail, not someone who is dancing. There is only one other clearly defined melodic idea in the first phrase (measure 3—x), and it is mechanically copied four times. In music to be listened to, repeating this idea four times would be about two times too many. However, in music for dancing, this kind of repetition causes no problem at all. It is lively, rhythmic, and predictable and keeps the dance moving forward without upsetting the musical flow in any way that might throw off the dancers. (Though it is probably just a happy coincidence, the fact that the last two notes of the phrase are the same as the first two reinforces the clarity of the form, as the listener hears the same two notes, A–D, end the first phrase and begin the repeat.)

If popular dance music is all about clear articulated structure, then the way this B section begins could not be more perfect. Contrast with the first phrase is provided in utterly "gettable" fashion by having the whole B section switch to a higher register, essentially an octave above the A section. (Like switching from alto to soprano.) This register shift is made perfectly clear by beginning the B section with a repeat of the opening idea an octave higher. (Repeating the opening here serves more as a structural marker than a development of the idea in any real sense.) The A section's only other idea—the one in measure 3—makes two additional appearances, more out of simply being compositionally "available" than out of any real desire to develop the thought, while the last four measures bring in a new idea (*y*) to let the dancers know that the end will be coming when they hear this music the next time around. The final two measures literally stop the dance by bringing the dancers up short with a rhythm that emphasizes the second beat of the measure (like a reversed foot in poetry) for the only time in the piece. This perfectly clear final gesture ends this highly effective piece of dance music.

For the purposes of this chapter, this minuet is as interesting for what it is not as for what it is. What a dancer/listener notices in this minuet first and foremost are the key points of demarcation at the beginning and end of each section. Then he notices the overall rhythmic flow and, most important, the experience of hearing each section twice ‖:A:‖ ‖:B:‖. There are no significant musical events within the course of each phrase that stop the musical flow, and there is no motivic development, increase or decrease of tension, or melodic climax designed to capture the attention of the listener in mid-phrase. This is a classic two-repeat form.

A "Listen-to" Minuet

Let's compare this Playford minuet to a minuet of Handel's from the same time period—the D Major Minuet from *Water Music*.

EXAMPLE 56

[continued]

EXAMPLE 56 [continued]

Like the Playford minuet, Handel's is a classic, two-repeat form. Though one could surely dance to this music, and the royal boating party in 1717 that Handel wrote it for might well have involved dancing, the kinds of subtle details the piece contains are ultimately designed to be listened to. In the spirit of the Playford minuet, I have written a more conventional, less interesting version of Handel's opening phrase.

EXAMPLE 57

Instead of my rhythmically plodding version, which opens with ten quarter notes in a row, Handel's faster notes in the second measure immediately give life to the phrase while retrospectively (by being different) turning the opening four repeated notes (*x*) into an idea. Measures 3 and 4 in both the Handel version and mine already begin to work with four repeated notes, but in contrast to my boring version, Handel's has a fantastic trill on the fourth note, followed by a snappy resolution and a repeat of the whole lively version lower, in measures 5 and 6. In addition, though we cannot know its significance yet, while my uninspired ending to the phrase simply symmetrically copies the opening (measures 7 and 8), Handel's version decorates it with faster eighth notes (*x* varied). Only in the B section will we discover the significance of this seemingly insignificant variation.

In music like this, something interesting is happening at every moment, demanding to be noticed. Details like the ones I have just described tend to occur only in "listen-to" music. If every piece of music embeds in its content a belief about the identity of its audience and what they will or will not be able to follow, this piece believes in an audience that is paying attention. To be more precise, not only paying attention, but remembering, as the B section shows. Unlike the composer of the Playford minuet, Handel begins his B section by working with ideas from his A section, immediately creating contrast by thinning out the orchestration and eliminating the brass for four measures. At the same time, a brand-new idea is created by combining the idea of four repeated notes (measure 9) and our "varied ending" (measures 11 and 12). When this idea is answered by the full orchestra in call-and-response fashion (measures 13 through 16), the varied ending again concludes the thought. What had seemed like a momentary detail when it ended the A section has now turned out to be a structural marker ending every thought.

Whether the resemblance is coincidental or whether Handel actually knew the Playford minuet, the key figure of Handel's final phrase (measure 17 through the end) is an exact, note-for-note copy of measures 13 and 14 (the *y* phrase) of the Playford minuet. Since copying was routine in the Baroque era, no contemporary listener would have cared, but proprietorship issues aside, what is instructive is how differently the two composers use the same notes. In the Playford minuet, the figure is simply part of an ongoing melodic flow. It is not highlighted in any way, and it calls no real attention to itself.

Handel, however, turns the figure into an idea by repeating it, and then varies its third repetition to lead to an ending. For a "compared-to-what" listener, this ending is superb. Handel takes the original varied ending from measures 7 and 8, where the melody was a less-than-final F♯ (remember our earlier discussion of the degrees of finality of different cadences), and makes it more final to end the piece by repeating it with a D in both melody and bass.

Though as noted earlier, one could probably dance to this minuet if there was enough room on the king's barge, it is surely "listen-to" music from beginning to end. The piece will simply not permit itself to become background music. However, though every measure has musical worth, the fundamental form, as in the Playford minuet, is still defined by its end points. The music drives toward these section-ending cadences, which provide the only pauses in the narrative flow. Like the Playford minuet, the piece still consists of two parts, two portions of music, and the listener's overall experience of the form is still defined by hearing each portion twice.

A Classical-Period Minuet

If we skip from the first quarter of the eighteenth century to the last—from the Baroque world to the Classical world—everything has changed. Of all the dance forms in the Baroque period, only the minuet survived to become a regular part of Classical-period music. Though on the surface both the minuet and its middle section, called the *trio*, are still two-repeat forms, their interior content has changed in ways that alter the fundamental meaning and experience of the form. Let's use a minuet from one of Haydn's superb late string quartets as a way of entering the form. Here is the minuet portion of the minuet-and-trio movement from Haydn's String Quartet, op. 76, no. 1.

EXAMPLE 58

[continued]

EXAMPLE 58 [continued]

Like the Playford and Handel minuets, Haydn's minuet is a clear two-repeat form, but the inner content is now completely different. First of all, the kind of intense, ongoing development of the musical possibilities contained in a single motive that we will find at the heart of sonata form (see chapter 10) has now invaded the world of the minuet, and this new purpose has become as important to the listener's experience of the form as its two-repeat structure. Haydn's entire minuet grows out of its first three notes. If you simply look at the first two melody notes in each of the first six measures of the piece, the fundamental idea, or topic, of the minuet immediately becomes clear. Every measure begins with two-repeated notes preceded by a pickup note. For the purposes of our discussion, I will call this three-note idea "And Re-peat." If you quickly scan the entire minuet, you will see that thirty-three of its forty measures begin with two repeated notes. This kind of sonatalike fixation on the developmental possibilities of a single idea changes the entire narrative flow of the minuet. Though on one level this piece is still about the symmetrical repetitions of two portions of music, it is also about an obsessive exploration of the developmental possibilities of "And Re-peat."

Without getting into all of the wonderful details in this minuet, suffice it to say that much of its compositional ingenuity depends on varying the interval between "And" and "Re" and between "peat" and "And." The entire piece turns brilliantly on two particular developments of this idea, and one speck of a contrasting idea. On the most obvious, surface level, the key dramatic moment in the A section is the shocking switch to *fortissimo* in measure 8. Playing loud, fast eighth notes after seven quiet measures of quarter notes is a simple way to produce an effect, but something much wittier and more sophisticated is going on as well. The eighth notes in measure 8 (and in the corresponding place in measure 36) are the only "fast" notes in the entire minuet, and they sound utterly surprising when we first hear them, but preparation is actually made in two subtle ways. If you look at the cello part, beginning in measure 1, you will immediately see that the accompaniment has been gradually speeding up (if anything can be "gradual" in this fast tempo) from one note per measure in measures 1 through 4, to two per measure in measures 5 and 6, then three in measure 7, leading finally to five per measure in the *fortissimo* bar.

The preparation for the *fortissimo*, however, is not only rhythmic but melodic as well. Though the motive in measure 8 sounds and feels new, it is really just a decoration of "And Re-peat" with inserted eighth notes. E. M. Forster said that "a rounded character in fiction must be surprising in convincing ways," and the preparation for this moment has been made so carefully that it sounds both surprising and convincing.

Because the A section ends while we are still recovering from the shock of the *fortissimo*, we barely notice the final notes of the phrase. But Haydn notices everything. As in Handel's minuet, the A section's two final bars actually contain the only other melodic idea in the piece—an idea that will be instantly recognizable each of the four times it occurs because it contains the only measure in the minuet that does not begin with two repeated notes. To be utterly precise, this six-note concluding idea begins on the last note of measure 8, and it is actually a descending four-note scale leading to two repeated notes (measure 10) to finish the phrase. I will call this ending, "And 1 2 3 Re-peat."

Before we get to the second part of Haydn's two-repeat form, we can already learn a great deal by observing what has been kept and what has been changed in this unquestionably "listen-to" minuet. On the simplest external level, as in both the Playford and Handel min-uets, the A section is short and immediately repeats. It is interesting that even when the second halves of Classical-period minuets begin to expand, the first halves almost invariably remain short. Like those in the Playford and Handel minuets, Haydn's A section still pushes toward a clear structural arrival at its end point, but the way in which it does so points up the changes in the style. For Haydn, the push to the cadence is now dramatic and surprising. The eighth notes are a surprise, the *fortissimo* is a surprise, and this dramatic outburst turns the opening into a wonderfully irregular ten-measure phrase instead of a conventional eight-measure phrase. Dancing the minuet to this music would be inconceivable. The tempo (presto) alone would make it ridiculous to even try, while the shocking *fortissimo* and confusing, irregular phrase structure would surely lead to a mutiny on the dance floor. It is not only the tempo of the actual music that has sped up, however, it is the speed of the musical thought as well. Where once it might have been the dancer's legs that were tired at the end of a minuet, now it is the listener's ears, and the second half of the piece pushes these developments to the breaking point.

The B section begins by stringing together four versions of the opening idea to make a new shape—a rising scale over repeated D's in the cello (measures 11 through 14). The D's seem harmless at the moment, but an experienced Haydn listener is always suspicious. All of a sudden (in measure 14), Haydn starts to work with "And 1 2 3 Re-peat"—played legato (connected), not short and separated as before. This leads directly to the kind of fantastic moment that, if you are listening for plot, truly defines what makes Haydn great. Until measure 19, there have been no pauses in the melody (no rests), and every group of repeated notes has been preceded by a pickup note (the "And" before "Re-peat"). Then, in measure 19, Haydn reduces the motive to its essence, just the two repeated notes, by removing the pickup note. "And Re-peat" gets reduced to "Re-peat" . . . "Re-peat" . . . "Re-peat." However, this is not just the essence of the opening motive, it is the essence of the entire piece, since "Re-peat," the two repeated notes, is what the piece's two ideas have in common. As if this is not enough to pay attention to at one time, the cello (in measure 19) turns the single D's from measures 11 through 14 into a two-note idea by adding a pickup note on the way back to the three-note idea that began the piece: "And Re-peat."

We are now at the center of the piece's universe (measures 21 through 23), its core moment. The melody has "Re-peat" . . . "Re-peat" . . . "Re-peat" but can't find its pickup note. The cello has "And Re" . . . "And Re" . . . "And Re" but can't find "peat." The music gets softer (diminuendos) as our listening gets more intense, and then in a fantastic stroke, the violin takes the cello's D–D ("And Re"), alters its second note, and adds a third, turning it into D–G–G to return to the opening melody (compare measures 1 through 4 with measures 23 through 26). "And Re" has found "peat"!

After the opening four measures are repeated in measures 23 through 26, the rest of the minuet is a highly modified version of the A section. As we are on the verge of becoming completely lost (i.e., unable to compare what we are hearing to what happened in the A section), the *fortissimo* eighth notes return with a shock and seem to end the piece in measure 38 with the same music that ended the A section. Symmetrical and satisfying. Minuet over. But not quite! In a final touch that only could have been written by Haydn, just as the audience is getting ready to applaud after the resounding *fortissimo* ending in measure 38, almost as an afterthought, two witty, soft bars of "Re-peat, Re-peat" add an extra, surprise ending. And if that's not fantastic enough, as a bonus for the listener with a superb memory, these final three measures are actually a quotation of the three chords that opened the entire quartet two movements earlier.

Two Parts or Three Parts?

Embedded within all of the fantastic detail in this minuet is a new approach to two-repeat form. In both the Playford and Handel examples, the core of the listening experience was hearing two portions of music, each symmetrically repeated. Musical flow was continuous and pushed toward the cadence points at the end of each section. No event in the middle of either section came close to the structural significance of the cadences that ended each section, and no complete segments of music from the A section were repeated in any wholesale way in the B section. In Haydn's minuet, however, as in nearly all Classical-period minuets, the return of the opening music in the middle of the B section is a central defining fact of the form. The B section is no longer a single unit of music; it is now divided at the return of A. Instead of ‖:A:‖ ‖:B:‖, we now have ‖:A:‖ ‖:BA:‖ or ‖:A:‖ ‖:BA′:‖ (A′ is the symbol for a variation, here referring to A). A two-part form—two portions of music, both repeated—now contains a three-part ABA form within it. This is far more than just a shift of diagrams and letters. The fundamental listening experience of "home–away–home" that we saw in the thirty-two-bar song form is now a component of our two-part form. From the moment the second, or B, section of Haydn's minuet starts, in measure 11, we are, in a sense, preparing to come "home"; not only to the opening theme at measure 23 but to the opening key as well. To return to the opening key and music at the same time makes for a highly articulated moment of structural arrival, and this moment of return becomes more and more dramatic as the classical period progresses.

Three-part ABA form affects not only the form of the minuet itself but also the form of its accompanying trio (the minuet's middle section) and the overall shape of the entire movement as well. The trio is customarily in the same two-part ‖:A:‖ ‖:BA:‖ form as the minuet, though it tends to be simpler in texture and content. The term *trio* as the name for the middle section of a Classical-period minuet actually comes from "the seventeenth-century custom of writing minuets and other dances in three parts, frequently for two oboes and bassoon, a treatment that was used particularly for the second of two dances played alternately, resulting in the arrangement Menuet, Menuet en trio, Menuet" (*Harvard Dictionary of Music*). In a complete Classical-period minuet-and-trio, the minuet is played once with both sections repeated, followed by the trio played once, also with both sections repeated, followed by a return to the minuet played through without repeats. "Home–away–home" operates on every structural level. The minuet's form is ‖:A:‖ ‖:BA:‖, the trio's form is ‖:A:‖ ‖:BA:‖, and the complete overall form—minuet-trio-minuet—is ABA. A fundamental new listening principle has entered the world of the minuet because the fundamental purpose the minuet serves has changed. "Dance-to" music has become "listen-to" music as part of a seismic cultural shift affecting every aspect of musical life, a shift symbolized by the central form at the heart of the period: sonata form.

[10]

Sonata Form

A Story in Three Acts

Oral or written stories are told in three parts. More commonly called "Three Acts." . . . The beginning, Act One is the situation. The middle, Act Two, the complications. The end, Act Three, the conclusion.

—LEW HUNTER, *SCREENWRITING 434*

Sonata form arose at a watershed moment in the history of classical music. As Charles Rosen explains in *The Romantic Generation*, before the Classical period, pure instrumental music was actually a genre of minor significance. Vocal music, in particular religious music and opera, was what mattered most. It was no accident that the rise of instrumental music as its own independent form coincided with the rise of the public concert. It was one thing to use pure instrumental music for functional purposes, say as background music for dancing a minuet. But for instrumental music to truly stand alone, as something to be listened to without words or a function to support it, it needed to have something compelling to hold the listener's attention, and the dramatic narrative of sonata form fit the bill perfectly.

It is important to keep in mind that, as I mentioned earlier, sonata form as a description or as a recipe for writing sonatas was created by theorists looking backward after the fact. Though there is dispute about who first coined the term, Carl Czerny claimed to have been the first to use it, around 1840, long after Haydn, Mozart, and Beethoven were dead. So if Haydn, Mozart, and Beethoven were not following a recipe or a description, where then did these narrative forms come from? Rosen points out that "the original meaning of 'sonata' was 'played' as opposed to 'sung,' and it only gradually acquired a more specific, but always flexible sense . . . Sonata is not a definite form like a minuet or a French overture: it is, like the fugue, a way of writing, a feeling for proportion, direction, and texture rather than a pattern." But if sonata is not a definite form but rather a way of writing, what is that "way of writing"? Are there fundamental narrative principles that shape the way a sonata's musical story is told?

Three-Act Stories

If you look at descriptions of storytelling structure in other plot-based genres like detective novels and screenplays, it is striking how similar their underlying narrative principles seem to be, not only to each other but to sonatas as well. Lew Hunter's screenwriter's manual, *Screenwriting 434*, puts the basic formula clearly: "Oral or written stories are told in three parts. More commonly called 'Three Acts.' . . . The beginning, Act One is *the situation*. The middle, Act Two, *the complications*. The end, Act Three, *the conclusion*." Even jokes seem to fall into this same, simple three-part structure. As Sol Saks puts it in *Funny Business: The Craft of Comedy Writing*, "Every humorous anecdote, every two-line joke, is a story and follows the three-act construction—situation, development, resolution." On the most schematic level, like screenplays, detective novels, and jokes, sonata form tells a three-act story. Act I, "the situation," is the *exposition*, in which the composer "exposes," or introduces, the main themes or plot elements. Act II, "the complications," is the *development*, in which the themes develop; the plot thickens. Act III, "the resolution," is the *recapitulation*, where the exposition's themes return with tensions and structural issues resolved.

In the most general sense, in terms of basic structure, sonata form is essentially identical to minuet form, ‖:A:‖ ‖:BA:‖, with the ‖:A:‖ section expanded in length and content to become the exposition, and the ‖:BA:‖ section expanded to become the development and recapitulation. (The A section is still repeated in nearly all Classical-period sonatas, though not necessarily in later nineteenth-century sonatas, while the ‖:BA:‖ section is rarely repeated, for reasons we will address later in this chapter.) But though sonata form may have grown out of minuet form both historically and formally, its new dramatic shape and purpose involved much more than simply expanding the size and proportions of an already existing form. To understand this striking new way of writing, we must first step back and get a grasp of two key concepts at the heart of the form—key and modulation.

Musical Travel: Key and Modulation

Though a detailed technical discussion of key and modulation is beyond the scope of this book, getting a feel for what these two concepts fundamentally mean and how they work in sonata form is vital to grasping its core dynamic. Here is a quick theory lesson for non-musicians. If you look at the keyboard of a modern piano, each octave contains seven white and five black keys arranged as follows:

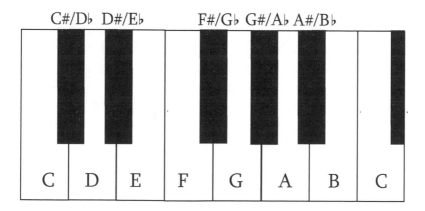

The distance from any key to its nearest key above or below is a half step. Two half steps equal a whole step. All scale systems, including the major and minor scales at the heart of tonality, are particular arrangements of whole and half steps, and these patterns can be reproduced starting on any note. (For the purposes of this basic discussion, I exclude scales that use non-Western tuning systems with quarter tones and the like.) If you simply go up the keyboard from C to C using only white keys (C–D–E–F–G–A–B–C), you have the pattern of a C major scale. W–W–H, W–W–W–H. ("W" equals a whole step, "H" equals a half step). The same pattern of whole and half steps beginning and ending on a D would be a D-major scale, and so on. In the most limited sense of the term *key*, if a piece of music is said to be "in the key of C major," the chords that are available "in the key" are the ones you can make by combining the notes of the C-major scale. The two most important chords in any key—the pillars of tonal music—are the chords based on the *home note* (the tonic) and the fifth note (the dominant). In the key of C, the note C is the main note, or "tonal center," of the piece, and it is the center or magnet to which all the other notes and chords are drawn.

A minor scale also contains seven notes but with its own unique arrangement of whole steps and half steps: W–H–W, W–W–W–H. (There are slightly different patterns for what musicians call "harmonic" minor scales and "melodic" minor scales, but the difference is not important for the purposes of this discussion.) A key is called major or minor according to whether it is based on the major or minor scale. Because there are a limited number of musical possibilities using only the seven notes of a scale (though far more than one might think), tonal pieces of almost any significant length invariably use notes outside their keys, called *accidentals*, and ultimately travel to other keys as well, temporarily leaving the home key behind. A piece in C major, for example, might travel, or *modulate*, to the key of G major, which means that the notes and chords of a G-major scale would temporarily become "home," with G as the new tonic note. The more notes two keys have in common, the more *closely related* they are said to be. So C major (C–D–E–F–G–A–B) and G major (G–A–B–C–D–E–F♯) are closely related keys as they share six of their seven notes. The fewer notes two keys have in common,

the more *remote* they are said to be—C major and F♯ major
(F♯–G♯–A♯–B–C♯–D♯–E♯) are remote keys as they have only one
note in common. As a painting with perspective has a central vanish-
ing point that organizes its visual space, a piece of tonal music has a
central point, the tonic note, which organizes its musical space, creating a continuum of relationships in which keys are relatively nearer
or more remote from the home key.

The reason all of this is so important is that the movement away
from the home key and the eventual return to it is integral to sonata
form. It is a driving force behind the entire form. From the moment
the home key is left behind, no matter what happens thematically or
melodically, on the most basic level, we are always waiting to return
to it. The longer we spend "away," and the more remote the key or
keys we travel to, the greater our desire to return "home." The journey of "home–away–home" is one of the fundamental movements
that shape sonata form, but it is the way this harmonic journey inter-
acts with each sonata's thematic and melodic narrative that creates its
particular plot.

Let's use a "textbook" sonata-form movement by Beethoven to
see how it tells its three-act story, section by section, and act by
act, always remembering that narrative principles and storytelling
strategies, rather than fixed, ex-post-facto rules, shape these musical
plots.

Act I: The Exposition

*The tonic is established by means of a harmonically clear-cut
primary theme or themes. After this section comes a more
vigorous or brilliant transition that accomplishes the modulation
to the new key. In order to confirm or stabilize the new key, the
composer may introduce one or more contrasting secondary
themes. The exposition then closes with cadential material,
which may range from conventional chordal passages to full-
fledged themes.*

—HARVARD DICTIONARY OF MUSIC

EXAMPLE 59

"The tonic is established by means of a harmonically clear-cut primary theme or themes." Though Beethoven had no copy of the *Harvard Dictionary of Music* to follow, this early piano sonata of his (op. 14, no. 2) follows the recipe exactly. It begins with a graceful six-note idea (*x*) that has a "clear-cut," well-defined shape. The idea is immediately repeated so we know it's an idea, and then it's repeated twice a step higher to further cement the shape in our ear. The second half of the phrase (measures 5 through 7) leaves the six-note motive behind and begins to push gently toward the cadence in measure 8. Notice how every element coordinates to create this push. The melody, instead of working with the opening, leisurely, six-note motive, starts working with a shorter, more urgent, three-note idea (measures 6 through 7). At the same time, the left hand, which had serenely played only three notes per measure in each of the first four measures (all over the same G "pedal note"), now becomes more active, with six notes in every measure. A perfect authentic cadence resolves the phrase on the downbeat of measure 8 with utter harmonic clarity. Flawlessly illustrating the textbook recipe, these first eight measures establish the home key, or tonic (G major), "by means of a harmonically clear-cut primary theme."

"After this section comes a more vigorous or brilliant transition that accomplishes the modulation to the new key." Though the section from measure 8 through measure 25 is not really "more vigorous or brilliant," it does accomplish the modulation to the new key. There are several important things to notice about this passage that are widely applicable to sonata-form movements of all kinds. Articulated structure is fundamental to the dramatic nature of sonata form. Major events like arrivals and departures nearly always receive clear highlighting and underlining. Notice the way that both the left hand and the right hand immediately let the listener know this transition section has begun. The right hand introduces a new motive: a measure of repeated notes plus a two-note "sigh" in measures 9 and 10 with the combination decorated and repeated in measures 11 and 12. The left hand at the same time begins continuous motion, subtly completing the acceleration from three, to six, to eight notes per measure, in effect saying, "We are under way, leaving home, heading somewhere new."

The transition to the new key could not be smoother. The key we are heading for in measure 26 is D major, but when a composer wants to make the arrival of a key an "event," he does not actually head for the tonic chord of that key but rather its dominant chord (here, A major) so that he can arrive conclusively with our familiar, key-defining, dominant-tonic, perfect authentic cadence ("The End"). If you look at the first note of each four-note group in the left hand from measure 8 through measure 19, you will see the bass move neatly up a scale from G–A–B–C–C♯–D–E–F–G–G♯ and finally A. Not only is the direction of the passage utterly clear, it is dramatic as well, as the pace doubles halfway through (in measure 14). After one chord for each two-measure group in measures 8 and 9, 10 and 11, and 12 and 13, the pacing speeds up to two chords per measure in measure 14. This coordinates perfectly with the right-hand melody, which articulates this moment of acceleration (in measure 14) by introducing a new two-measure idea (see motive γ in example 59). This is then shortened to one measure in measures 18 and 19 to create the final push to the dominant, A.

What happens next (in measures 19 through 26) is crucial to understanding sonata form. This entire transition section is ultimately heading for an arrival in the new key of D major in measure 26. Technically speaking, we have already reached the dominant, A, in measure 19 and could go right to the tonic, D, in measures 26 and 27. But as we have already seen, articulated structure is crucial to the drama of sonata form. A major event like the arrival of an exposition's second key requires highlighting and underlining, and that is the sole function of measures 19 through 25. They delay the arrival of the second key and let us know that something important is about to occur. They get us ready for an event. The music, which has no real thematic content, merely figuration, clearly reflects the exposition's structure. Learning to hear the difference between "theme-establishing" passages, transitional passages, and passages of preparation is an important step in learning to follow the narrative of sonata form.

Act I: Part II

"In order to confirm or stabilize the new key, the composer may introduce one or more contrasting secondary themes." Once again, the music here is perfectly designed to reflect the structure. The arrival in the new key is a major harmonic event in an exposition, and it is almost invariably marked by a thematic event of some kind that articulates the structure.

Though Haydn is more likely to present a varied version of his opening idea at this moment than a new one, introducing a contrasting theme is a natural way to dramatize this arrival. How this moment is turned into a dramatic element in the sonata-form narrative will be different for each composer and each piece. The fact that this moment offers dramatic storytelling potential is what is important.

EXAMPLE 60

Beethoven's sonata offers a graceful example of a contrasting theme used to "confirm or stabilize the new key." The theme itself also offers a reminder of how important repetition is to listener comprehension. Within three measures (measures 26 through 28), the two fundamental gestures of this second theme are cemented in the listener's ear. (The term *second theme* can be confusing. It is generally used to refer specifically to the theme that marks the arrival of the second key, though it might actually be the fourth, fifth, or sixth theme heard in the piece. Adding to the confusion, the entire section of music in the second key that begins with the second theme is often referred to as the second theme group or second group.) The opening right-hand two-note figure with its elegant long-short rhythm is immediately repeated three times. (Note how the left hand repeats its figure as well, an octave higher each time.) The listener "gets" the gesture instantly. The rest of the idea (measures 27 and 28) is also utterly clear and rhythmically distinct—descending two-note "sighs" moving down the scale in sixteenth notes—and six repetitions ensure that the listener will "get" this gesture as well. When the second half of the melody (measures 30 through 32) repeats the first half transposed lower, not only has the new key been stabilized, the new melody has been confirmed as well. The harmonic plot and the melodic plot are perfectly coordinated to articulate the exposition's dramatic shape.

"The exposition then closes with cadential material, which may range from conventional chordal passages to full-fledged themes." Closing passages—passages that "wrap things up"—are an important component of sonata form. Because closing passages are designed to conclude and resolve sections, repetition, a key structural stabilizer, frequently plays a central role.

EXAMPLE 61

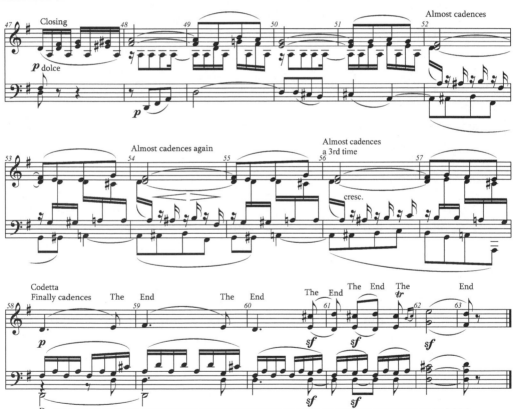

A leisurely phrase beginning at measure 47 begins to wind things down and almost reaches a cadence at measure 52. However, simply cadencing here would not be a sufficiently dramatic, section-ending event for a sonata-form narrative. Like our earlier Mozart example, which made its final cadence conclusive through delay, Beethoven tries to cadence three times. His first attempt, at measure 52, is unsuccessful. In measures 54 and 55 he tries again and fails. The fourth time, however, he's successful, which is what makes the resolution at measure 58 feel so final.

In the same way that stopping a moving car smoothly is a gradual, not an instantaneous, process, closing passages frequently have multiple stages, and a final extension, or *codetta*, like the section from measures 58 through 63, is quite common. If you look at the left hand, this whole final passage is all over a held D. We are now "home" in our new key of D major. Above this D, everything is wrap-up music. The harmony repeats "The End" over and over again, and the melody repeats simple cadential figures of no thematic significance. All loose ends are neatly tied up. We are done. End of chapter. End of exposition.

Act II: The Development

As in a minuet, nearly all Classical-period sonatas repeat their entire expositions. We have already seen in chapter 3 that repeating a phrase or a section lets the listener know that the entire phrase or section is a unit. Repetition allows the listener to grasp the music the second time through as a single thought. This is precisely the function of repeating the exposition in sonata form. Listening forward the first time through, not knowing how things will turn out, we are meeting the themes, transitions, keys, and closing sections for the first time. Only the second time through do we grasp the entire exposition as a single compared-to-what unit that we can bring forward with us to the rest of the piece. It is also important to remember that unlike a listener today, who is familiar with the core classical repertoire through recordings and may be hearing the repeat of the exposition of a well-known piece like the *Jupiter* Symphony or the *Eroica* Symphony for the two hundredth time, for Classical-period listeners hearing this music for the first time, the repeat of the exposition was their single chance to become familiar enough with this material to be able to follow the variations and developments they were about to hear in upcoming sections. Sonata form assumes that two times through the exposition is both essential and sufficient to produce the listener memory required to follow future plot developments.

A quick word on terms. It is important not to confuse the use of the word *development* to describe the process of elaborating or varying a musical idea with its use as a label describing the middle section of a sonata-form movement. The process of development occurs in nearly all forms of music, and thematic development in sonata-form movements is by no means limited to the "development section" proper. (Remember our Haydn quartet example.) The development section of a sonata-form movement, however, works on developing the ideas of the exposition in a particularly focused way and combines this motivic work with harmonic exploration as well. Here is the first portion of Beethoven's development section.

EXAMPLE 62

[continued]

EXAMPLE 62 [continued]

The development section ordinarily modulates still farther afield and provides varied and often dramatic treatment of material already heard in the exposition . . . applying such techniques as melodic variation, fragmentation, expansion or compression, contrapuntal combination, textural and contextual change, and reharmonization to one or many themes of the exposition.

— HARVARD DICTIONARY OF MUSIC

At heart, sonata-form development sections are explorations of the possibilities contained in a movement's musical ideas. Development sections explore material we have already heard from new angles and in new contexts in order to expand our sense of what these ideas mean. The first phrase of Beethoven's development section is a classic example. The graceful, elegant, six-note theme that opened the piece was in a major key. When the first four measures of the development section (measures 63 through 67) shift this opening theme into a minor key, its entire mood and meaning changes. It is as if we have suddenly caught a glimpse of our main character's darker side. The lighthearted, opening idea acquires a hint of sorrow, adding depth. The character transformation then intensifies through a classic example of *fragmentation.* Beethoven takes only the last four notes of the six-note idea and begins to work with this shortened fragment. He repeats it three times as the harmony underneath tries to find the correct key. This kind of intense focusing in on a small portion of a theme, working with its constituent parts, is at the heart of sonata-form development sections. Once Beethoven has reduced a theme to small molecular fragments, he is free to recombine these fragments in new ways, but he is always careful to make the process audible to the listener. Having reduced the six notes (G, G, D, E-flat, B, and C) to just the last four (D, E-flat, B, and C), he then keeps only the last three (E-flat, B, and C) and makes them the core of a "new" idea (F, **E-flat, B, C**, G♯, and A) imitated back and forth between the hands. Though the plot is thickening quickly, Beethoven makes sure we follow the narrative and hear the way the theme is taken apart and reassembled. Like the architects of modern buildings with exposed ventilation shafts and exposed plumbing, Beethoven wants us to see the structure, and to hear, step-by-step, how each new combination is made.

Having developed the first theme, Beethoven then starts to work with the second theme in measure 74. To make sure the listener follows the narrative, Beethoven repeats the first five measures of the second theme exactly as we heard them in the exposition, now simply transposed. But in measure 79, instead of continuing like the exposition, Beethoven gets "stuck" on the long-short figure while the left hand rises. The dynamics—*decrescendo* (getting softer) and *pianissimo*—reflect the drama of the moment. Where are we heading? How will this figure resolve?

After six repetitions, Beethoven slams into the remote key of A-flat major with a sudden shift to *forte*. (Again notice how everything coordinates to articulate this moment: The harmony shifts to A-flat major, the dynamic shifts to *forte*, a new triplet accompaniment figure begins in the right hand, and a new motive begins in the left.) Our opening six-note melody changes its first note, becomes a left-hand idea underneath continuous motion in the right hand, and develops a whole new ending (measures 84 and 85). Something completely new has been created out of our original material. Beyond any technical description, what is important about this section is hearing how Beethoven's graceful, elegant, opening theme has completely transformed its character. An idea we once thought we understood has shown completely new sides to its musical personality, forcing us to completely reevaluate our understanding. As we saw in chapter 1, some openings identify themselves right away. Others, like the one in this sonata, ask the listener to wait.

Though there are many wonderful details in this development section, in terms of gaining an understanding of the overall form, it is the way the development ends that is most important. Remembering that sonata form is fundamentally dramatic, with major structural events highlighted and underlined, the return to the opening material to begin the recapitulation, perhaps the key dramatic event in the second half of a sonata-form movement, nearly always receives special treatment. The *Harvard Dictionary of Music*'s definition of the final portion of the development section reads: *"A majority of development sections conclude with a passage known as a retransition, which sets the stage for the dramatic and dual return of the tonic key and original thematic material at the beginning of the recapitulation, usually by suspensefully stressing the dominant."* As we saw earlier, the easiest way to make a cadence or an arrival more conclusive is to delay it. In a sense, the entire development section functions harmonically as one long delay of the return to the opening key. Since the final step before that return will normally be an arrival on the dominant chord ("The"), prolonging that dominant during a passage called the *retransition* is the commonest way of making the actual return ("End") emphatic and dramatically effective. Even in this early Beethoven sonata, the retransition passage occupies nearly one third of the development section.

EXAMPLE 63

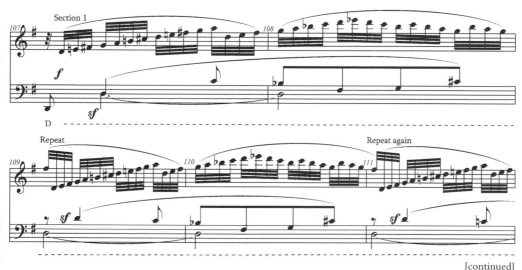

[continued]

EXAMPLE 63 [continued]

Since the sonata's home key is G major, the retransition is on the dominant (D), and if you look at the left hand throughout this entire retransition, you will see that the lowest note in all eighteen measures is a D (a "pedal point"). No matter what happens above this, the whole passage "means" D. This retransition falls into three sections. Thinking metaphorically for a moment, if you want something to look bright you put it next to something dark, and one of the commonest techniques in sonata-form pieces in a major key is to write the retransition passage in a minor key, so that when the opening returns in a major key it will sound fresh and bright by comparison. Section one of this retransition (measures 107 through 114) does just that by using a repeating, minor-key scale figure to seemingly prepare the listener for a minor key return. Section two (measures 115 through 120) heightens our sense of anticipation and foreshadows the recapitulation by working with a core fragment drawn from the main theme: notes 3, 4, 5, and 6 of the minor-key version that began the development section. This is the first step in a classic Beethoven moment. The four-note fragment that is being worked with—the theme minus its first two notes—is made up of two half steps: G♯–A and E♯–F♯. The fragment tries to find its way back to the opening theme twice: G♯–A–E♯–F♯, G♯–A–E♯–F♯. That doesn't work, so Beethoven tries the same four-note fragment starting on a B six times (B–C–G♯–A), as if sheer insistent repetition might generate the return.

Then, in a stunning moment of explanation made utterly clear by eliminating the left hand completely, the same four-note fragment, now on D♯ (D♯–E–B–C), is reduced to two, two-note pairs, D♯–E and B–C. (The slurs connecting these notes make this absolutely clear.) Beethoven, on the verge of return, has reduced the theme to its core essence: a single half step. Once we are on this elemental level, every half step represents the entire piece. Measures 122 and 123 are a simple descent of half-step pairs—one of the most ordinary, mundane patterns in tonal music—but now these ordinary pairs have become carriers of the motivic essence of the entire piece. Even the final six-note scale that ends the passage is chromatic, that is, it is made up of half steps, and this scale "is" the piece as well. Everything is connected. Nothing is trivial. Everything is essential. The scale stops on C♯ and pauses. One more half step brings us to the D that begins the opening theme, and as "The" resolves to "End," our recapitulation begins.

Act III: The Recapitulation

The recapitulation starts with the return of the first theme in the home key. The rest of this section recapitulates (repeats) the exposition as it was first played except that the second group and closing theme appear in the home key. Longer works are rounded off by a coda.

—*HARVARD DICTIONARY OF MUSIC*

Recalling our simple three-act description of sonata form, Act III, "the resolution," is the recapitulation. Though it may be true, technically speaking, that what tends to occur in recapitulations is a return of the exposition's material with second group and closing theme music transposed to the home key, what is really important to understand is what this all has to do with resolution. Recapitulations do not simply repeat and transpose; they resolve compositional tensions and problems. The moment a sonata leaves the home key in a Classical-period sonata there is structural tension. No matter how long we may spend in a second or third key or how "acclimated" we may become to it, on the most fundamental level we always want to return "home."

Let me approach the overall structural movement of the form through a simple metaphor. Imagine that you are a native New Yorker with family and friends in the city and strong ties to the community. Your firm opens a Los Angeles branch, and asks you to move there for a year to start up a new office. You reluctantly agree, and from the moment you leave there is "structural tension." You are aware every moment in LA that you are "away," not "home." You gradually settle in, but six months into your year, the company asks you to spend your next six months setting up new offices in ever-more-remote cities, where you must adapt and vary your way of doing business because of diverse local situations. Some of these cities are in other countries, and the farther you travel from home, the more intense your desire to return. When you finally return to New York after a year away, your arrival at La Guardia airport (after considerable delay and circling—the retransition) is a highly significant moment. You are home. And being home, you must now sift through the experiences you had while you were away and make sense of them as you report to your boss and friends. You must decide what was important and what was not, what was essential and what was insignificant, and only by retelling that story at home do you discover what it means.

Though this example is obviously oversimplified and metaphorical, it illustrates fundamentally how sonata-form recapitulations work. In a sonata, all music that appears outside the home key is on the most basic level "dissonant." If the material is important, it can be resolved only by being played in the home key. But a sonata has thematic and structural tensions as well as harmonic ones. It is by no means a given that all of the material in an exposition is of equal importance. In Haydn's sonata-form movements, we rarely know what material is important, what is secondary, or what logical ordering of events makes sense until the recapitulation, where material is eliminated and reordered with breathtaking speed. In Beethoven's *Tempest* Sonata, we saw that it was unclear whether the slow, stop-start opening was even part of the main material of the movement, and only in the recapitulation did we discover its true role. A recapitulation must do more than simply "recap" events, it must interpret them while providing resolution to all of the piece's harmonic, thematic, and structural issues.

That being said, this Beethoven sonata has an almost textbook recapitulation befitting the simple material of the piece. The entire opening theme returns in the home key. The transition is effortlessly altered so that the "second group and closing theme appear in the home key," and a brief fourteen-measure coda rounds off the work by turning the opening theme into simple closing music. When the movement ends, all structural tensions—thematic, melodic, and harmonic—have been resolved. All is well in the sonata's world. Beethoven's three-act story is complete.

A Final Thought

In chapter 10 we saw that the minuet was both a two- and a three-part form. The same is true of sonata form, though the increase in length and drama impacts the form's underlying structure. Nearly all sonatas in the Classical period follow the minuet's example and repeat their first half, or exposition, thereby clearly articulating the form's overall division into two parts. However, very few sonata-form movements repeat their second halves the way minuets do. This is not simply because of the increase in length, but also because of a basic aesthetic shift already hinted at in the minuet. As sonata-form movements became more and more dramatic, with complex development sections that traveled farther and farther from home, the return to the home key and the opening music at the beginning of the recapitulation became a more and more significant event. The more suspenseful this moment became, the more inappropriate it seemed to repeat it. What was once an appropriate gesture of symmetry—repeating the second half of the piece—no longer made sense in a thoroughly dramatic form. Like the unveiling of the murderer in a mystery novel, certain narrative events can only happen once. As the proportions and dramatic content increased even more during the Romantic period, composers began to eliminate the exposition repeats as well, discarding what had become a vestigial organ from an earlier aesthetic.

Though for pedagogical purposes we have looked at sonata form in this chapter through the lens of its ex-post-facto recipe, it is imperative to remember once again that there was no fixed form or set of rules for writing a sonata-form movement. Storytelling patterns and procedures arose naturally as a response to recurring plot situations, and these patterns and procedures were imitated and varied from composer to composer and from piece to piece. They were also imitated from form to form. Though many Classical-period forms have different names—slow movement form, aria form, concerto form, rondo and sonata-rondo form—the underlying principles of sonata form are widely applicable to these forms as well. How composers handled the challenge of articulating and shaping the new dramatic structures they were beginning to create in sonata form influenced all the forms of the period. Yet as always, each piece created its own unique form as a response to its own unique content. Though the listening principles behind these forms might be general, all sonata forms are ultimately unique.

[11]

Passacaglia, Chaconne, and Fugue
Out of One, Many

Strength, says Leonardo da Vinci, is born of constraint and diesin freedom.

—IGOR STRAVINSKY

In *Poetics of Music* Stravinsky wrote,

> The more art is controlled, limited, worked over, the more it is free. My freedom thus consists in my moving about within the narrow frame that I have assigned myself for each one of my undertakings. I shall go even farther: my freedom will be so much the greater and more meaningful the more narrowly I limit my field of action and the more I surround myself with obstacles. The more constraints one imposes the more one frees oneself of the chains that shackle the spirit.

Stravinsky's provocative idea that constraint in art produces freedom is at the heart of this chapter. Like sonnets, haikus, villanelles, and other highly restrictive poetic forms, each of the three musical forms we will discuss next has a built-in technical challenge or constraint. In each form, some element is deliberately held fixed for virtually the entire duration of the piece. How to turn this creative constraint into an aesthetic opportunity is the composer's challenge. How to create variety in a form dominated by unity. How to create the many out of the one.

An Obstinate Bass

As with the forms we have looked at in the preceding chapters, I am not interested in comprehensively exploring each form's possibilities (an effort that would require an entire book for each form), but rather in getting at the basic listening principles and musical logic embedded in these forms. How does a fugue, a passacaglia, or a chaconne work? What is it like to experience these forms? It is interesting that although the first form we are going to discuss, the passacaglia, emerged in the seventeenth century, it was also used widely in the twentieth century—by Britten, Alban Berg, and Webern, among others—and continues to be a valuable, creative tool for many twenty-first-century composers, such as John Corigliano and Thomas Adès. What is it about the passacaglia's musical logic that allows composers four centuries apart to still find fresh possibilities in the form?

The terminology surrounding the words *passacaglia* and *chaconne* can be extremely confusing. Though it is possible to make clear textbook distinctions between these terms, composers during the Baroque period used them indiscriminately and interchangeably. Regardless of terms and labels, when listening to this music the single most important question to ask is always, "What stays the same, and what changes?" "What is fixed, and what is free?" And most important, "How does what is free continually change our understanding of what is fixed?"

The use of a repeating bass melody—the fixed element in a passacaglia—can be found in compositions as far back as the thirteenth century, but it becomes a prominent feature in a great deal of vocal and instrumental music in the seventeenth century. Sometimes the repeating bass melody is referred to as a *basso ostinato*, from the Italian meaning "obstinate bass." Sometimes it is called a *ground bass*. In spite of the interchangeability of the terms *passacaglia* and *chaconne* during the Baroque period, modern theorists call a composition based on a recurring bass melody a passacaglia and a composition based on a recurring set of harmonies a chaconne. "Dido's Lament" from Purcell's *Dido and Aeneas*, an aria in which the grieving Dido, betrayed by her lover,

Aeneas, bids farewell to her maid, Belinda, and to life itself, is one of the most famous and beautiful passacaglias ever written. The mood of impending death is created instantly by this stark *basso ostinato*.

EXAMPLE 64

[continued]

EXAMPLE 64 [continued]

[continued]

EXAMPLE 64 [continued]

"Dido's Lament"

The aria begins with an unaccompanied statement of the piece's ten-note ground bass. Many Baroque pieces use identical or similar ground basses, and this classic, often-used pattern makes a satisfyingly clear, self-contained journey within itself. It begins on the tonic, G, and moves down by half steps to the dominant, D, then finishes with a four-note close that leads to a perfect authentic cadence: D–G ("The End"). Notice the superb way that rhythm sets off this cadence. After three pairs of short-long rhythms (S/L S/L S/L), we finish with short, short-long, long (S/SL/L). The change in the rhythmic pattern and the two final long notes beautifully reinforce the cadence. (Clap the rhythm to really feel this.)

Once the bass has established its pattern, it repeats it identically eight times. That is the central fact of the composition. Unity in a passacaglia is a given. The challenge for the composer is to find a way to take the identical journey in the bass nine times, yet somehow make each journey different. One of the most significant challenges for Purcell in dealing with this particular ground bass is the fact that it cadences decisively every five measures, thereby threatening to stop all forward motion at each cadence. All passacaglia composers must be masters of elision—the art of avoiding and overlapping cadences—and Purcell superbly knits multiple statements of the ground bass together to create larger sections with a powerful overall shape instead of nine, short, self-contained units.

If a piece's bass line is fixed, much of its expression depends on its melody, and Purcell's is heartrending. Great song and aria composers do not set words to music, they set the emotions behind the words.

Purcell does not set "When I am laid in earth" to music, he sets the pain Dido feels as the image of her being "laid in earth" floats before her mind. All of the musical details grow out of that emotion. He could easily have set the first four measures like this.

EXAMPLE 65

Unlike my flat version of "laid" in measure 7, Purcell's vocal line has a beautiful, painful suspension (a tied or repeated note that becomes dissonant and then resolves) on the downbeat, or the first beat of the measure, which only resolves on the second note. When Dido completes the image with the words "am laid in earth," not only does the descending scale literally depict her being put into the grave, the halting rhythm (as opposed to my even rhythm) depicts her spasms of emotion as she reacts to the image.

No musical instrument is more sensitive to differences of register and range than the human voice, and Purcell's awareness of this is central to how this piece works. Following the comma after "earth," Purcell leaps to a higher register to differentiate the music of the grave from the music of the next phrase, "May my wrongs create / No trouble in thy breast." The higher register raises the emotional intensity of the scene, while the push to the vocal line's highest note of the phrase (E-flat in measure 11) masterfully elides the first cadence. Though the ground bass finishes its pattern and cadences on the downbeat of measure 11, the vocal phrase "May my wrongs create / No trouble in thy breast" continues right through the cadence and does not finish until the middle of the ground's next statement. One common way composers avoid the continual cadences of a ground bass is to write melodic phrases like Purcell's that last longer than the bass and cadence independently of it. When the voice finishes its melody in the middle of the bass phrase (measure 14), it allows the accompaniment to finish the rest of the ground alone, as Dido and the audience contemplate what she has just sung.

I have mentioned in several different contexts the fact that repeating an entire phrase lets the listener know that the multimeasure idea is a unit, and repetition is key to what happens next. In another superb elision, the cadence that ends the third statement of the ground bass (on the downbeat of measure 16) simultaneously begins a complete repeat of the entire vocal melody. The cadence is both an ending and a beginning, and when the whole first section repeats, we have the experience as a listener of hearing one large section of music—the opening done twice—rather than five individual statements of the ground bass.

"Remember Me"

The final section of this passacaglia is one of the most moving in all vocal music. The vocal line in the first part of the piece, while quite emotional, was essentially a continuous melody. Dido, though distraught, was still composed enough to be able to sing a long, beautifully shaped melodic line. However, in the final section of the piece, all composure vanishes. The text is an outcry, "Remember me, remember me." The vocal line is reduced to a four-note spasm on a single pitch. The harmonization of the ground bass, which fills in the space between the spasms, becomes more dissonant (taking up Dido's suspension from measure 6), as if the instrumental accompaniment has itself been affected by Dido's pain. As the piece begins to push toward its climax with the words "but ah! forget my fate," Purcell elides the end of the bass phrase skillfully. The melody pushes right past the cadence in measure 31 on its way to "fate" in measure 32, while the accompaniment supports this by adding a second chord at the beginning of measure 31 for the only time in the piece.

The climax is magnificent. The text repeats "Remember me" in measure 33, but now the four-note spasm goes up to a high G; the highest note in the entire piece. After the climax, the vocal music finishes with a superb depiction of resignation and acceptance as the melody finally resolves on the tonic note with the end of the ground for the first and only time. This final joining of Dido's melody with the ground bass seals her fate, and two more statements of the *basso ostinato* (note the superb harmony at measures 40 and 41 as Purcell avoids the normal dominant and normal tonic chords to elide the last two statements of the ground) end this tragic and poignant passacaglia.

Purcell's handling of the constraints of a *basso ostinato* throughout this aria could not be more masterful. Though the vocal portion of the piece covers six complete statements of the ground bass, the listener's experience is that of two large sections. Purcell uses elision, repetition, and register to knit multiple statements of the ground bass together, and he creates an overall shape and form for the piece that is informed at every moment by the repeating ground bass, but not determined by it. The repetitions of the *basso ostinato* give strength and unity to the vocal line without imprisoning it. As with a haiku, it is the interplay between what is strict and what is free that gives the piece its unique character, and this is not unconnected to the emotional content of the piece. Conveying Dido's powerful emotions as she confronts her imminent death through the rational, logical, constraining form of the passacaglia forces the expression to be contained and channeled. Like Dylan Thomas dealing with the powerful emotions brought up by his father's impending death through the complex, restrictive poetic form of the villanelle in "Do Not Go Gentle into That Good Night," sifting overwhelming feelings through the prism of highly logical, constraining forms can have a liberating effect, leading to potent, original expression.

Chaconne/Passacaglia, Passacaglia/Chaconne

I mentioned at the beginning of this chapter that the terms *passacaglia* and *chaconne* were used interchangeably during the Baroque period, and one of the reasons has to do with the fundamental interdependence of bass and harmony in Baroque music. The utterly central role of the bass line in the harmony of the period can be seen clearly in the shorthand notation called "figured bass" that composers used in the keyboard parts of the time. In this notation, only the left hand, or bass line, was written out, accompanied by a series of numbers or "figures" that told the harpsichordist which chords to play in the right hand. (A system not unrelated to the chord symbols used in today's popular-music "lead sheets.") What was primary was the actual bass line. The way the chords were to be arranged was up to the individual keyboard player to improvise. In a great deal of Baroque music, however, the bass line was written without any figures at all, because given the limited harmonic resources available, once the bass line was determined, in essence the harmony was determined as well. There simply were not that many chords you could put above any given bass

line that would make musical sense in the period's language. Consequently, once you chose a bass line, like the repeating bass line for a
passacaglia, you were essentially choosing a repeating set of harmonies
as well. And vice versa—choosing any clearly defined set of repeating harmonies usually generated an implicit bass line.

Anyone who has ever played the lower part of "Heart and Soul"
(the chords) over and over again as a friend improvised above knows
what a chaconne is. In "Heart and Soul" the recurring series of harmonies is the simple progression from C to A minor to F to G, but a
chaconne can be based on any recurring sequence of chords. Example 66 is the first sixteen measures of perhaps the most famous chaconne ever written, the fifth movement of Bach's Partita no. 2 in D
Minor for solo violin. In this monumental 257-measure work, Bach
restricts himself to nothing but four-bar units that always start on the
tonic and end on the dominant. However, as these first four statements of the pattern clearly show, although the piece is based on a
recurring set of harmonies, there is an implicit recurring bass line
(D–D–C#–D–Bb–G–A—marked with asterisks) as well. All of the
techniques of grouping and elision required to avoid motion-ending
cadences that we saw in Purcell's passacaglia are just as essential in
Bach's chaconne, and all of the listening principles we discussed with
respect to the passacaglia are applicable to the chaconne as well. Bass
and harmony, and forms based on repeating patterns in either, are intimately related in the Baroque world.

EXAMPLE 66

Modern Versions

It is interesting that both passacaglias and chaconnes have proved meaningful to a variety of composers in the twentieth and twenty-first centuries in very different kinds of music used for very different purposes. Jazz, rock, and various kinds of popular music have all been greatly influenced by a uniquely twentieth-century chaconne formula: the twelve-bar blues. This repeating harmonic pattern is based on the three basic chords that everyone who has ever played guitar learns first. In the key of C the basic twelve-bar pattern is C / C / C / C / F / F / C / C / G / F / C / C. Though many jazz musicians vary this simple pattern with extremely sophisticated substitute chords used in ingenious ways, it is the very familiarity and solidity of the twelve-bar chaconne formula that allows the listener to grasp and follow the elaborate decorations and variations.

But the chaconne has been used in the world of jazz for more than just creating twelve-bar blues. In a sense, the chaconne is the very basis of the way most jazz musicians treat well-known tunes, or "standards." The first time through the tune is played "straight," with the melody articulated in recognizable form over the tune's basic harmonies. In the solos that follow, the chords, or "changes" as they are called, are held fixed while the original melody is either intensively varied or completely disappears to be replaced by brand-new melodies that fit the underlying harmonies. As in a chaconne, what stays the same throughout all of the solos is the recurring harmonic pattern. What changes is everything else.

The passacaglia has also played a role in twentieth- and twenty-first-century classical music, and in a sense modern interest in the form has come about for reasons that are diametrically opposed to the original reasons the form arose. The very constraint that the form imposed on Baroque composers—how to create sufficient variety to counteract the unity created by a repeating pattern—was precisely what drew later composers to it. As contemporary musical languages proliferated, tonality weakened, and unifying principles had to be created from scratch for each piece. Consequently, the structure offered by a repeating bass line or a set of harmonies proved attractive to many composers.

(Chaconnes have been written by composers as diverse as Britten, Philip Glass, and John Adams, while passacaglias have been even more popular.) In Baroque music, a fixed bass line fundamentally dictated an underlying set of harmonies to match, but in the much more varied harmonic universe of the twentieth and twenty-first centuries, no such limitation existed. A repeating bass line like the one in Britten's passacaglia *Peter Grimes* (example 67) could be harmonized in an almost infinite number of ways. By itself, Britten's bass line is as clearly tonal as that of any Baroque passacaglia, yet its very clarity of key allows the upper parts to play against it. Though the ground bass is squarely in F major, at various points in the piece its final note, F, for example, is harmonized with A major, D-flat major, D minor, E-flat major, and E major chords, not to mention several other nontraditional chords. Each new harmonic combination changes the sound of the ground bass, as if viewing it from a different angle, like Claude Monet painting the same Rouen cathedral at different times of day in different lights.

In addition to the vastly expanded harmonic possibilities that twentieth-century music offered a passacaglia composer like Britten, twentieth-century rhythmic flexibility allowed for a treatment of the ground bass that would have been unthinkable in Baroque music. Though Britten's passacaglia is in standard 4/4 time with four beats to the measure, the ground-bass pattern is actually eleven beats long. This means that the first statement starts on beat 1, but the second statement starts in the middle of a measure on beat 4 (measure 3), the third statement on beat 3 (measure 6), and the fourth statement on beat 2 (measure 9); only on the fifth statement (measure 12) does the pattern again start on beat 1. Since it will always take four statements of the ground to return to beat 1 as a starting point, a four-statement grouping is instantly created, and since each note of the ground continually occurs in different parts of the measure, constantly changing harmony is assured. Regular phrases in the melody inevitably cadence at different points in the bass line's pattern, providing continual variety in the phrase structure as well as the harmony. The demands of unity and variety, similarity and contrast are reconciled in ways no Baroque composer could have ever imagined.

EXAMPLE 67

Fugue

Both passacaglias and chaconnes are forms "born of constraint."
Some recurring element—either a bass line or a set of harmonies—
is fixed and the composer's challenge is to make each repetition an
opportunity to hear the recurring element from a new angle, with
a new point of view. By putting a fixed element in continually new

contexts, variety is created out of unity. The many grows out of the one. The same thing is true of fugue. Like a passacaglia or a chaconne, a fugue has a recurring element—its main theme, called the *subject*—but the real interest for both the composer and the listener is not the continual return of the subject itself, but rather the way each return allows us to hear the subject anew by surrounding it with constantly changing music. Compared-to-what listening is the essence of fugue.

Unlike passacaglia and chaconne, fugue is not actually a form but rather a way of writing. Though many fugues use similar contrapuntal procedures (e.g., *inversion*—changing each ascending leap to a descending leap and vice versa; *diminution*—shortening each note of the subject rhythmically; and *augmentation*—lengthening each note of the subject), once a fugue finishes its opening section or exposition, no two fugues are alike. Because a fugue has no fixed form, discussion frequently focuses on various kinds of fugal devices like stretto (overlapping entries of the subject), augmentation, inversion, and the like, yet what is far more important is learning to hear and appreciate the art of counterpoint: the art of combining completely independent melodies in imaginative ways. To give you a feel for what great counterpoint is all about, I would like to compare a portion of two fugues that use virtually the identical subject: one by Johann Kaspar Ferdinand Fischer and one by Bach. Here are the first twenty-three measures of Fischer's E Major Fugue from a group of twenty preludes and fugues for organ entitled *Ariadne Musica*.

EXAMPLE 68

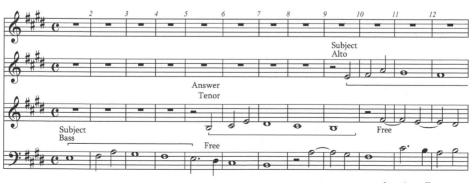

[continued]

EXAMPLE 68 [continued]

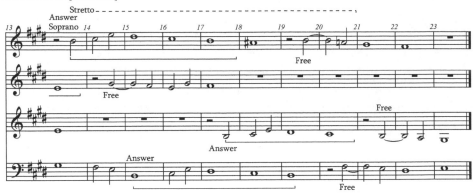

Fischer's Fugue

Though, as I have said, fugue is not a form, nearly all fugues begin with what is called an exposition: a section in which all the voices in the piece play the main idea or subject of the fugue. It is traditional in talking about fugues, even if they are written for instruments, to refer to the separate parts as "voices" and label the parts from lowest to highest as if they were choral parts: bass, tenor, alto, and soprano. Fischer's fugue has four voices and follows a common narrative strategy in expositions with entries rising in pitch from bass (measure 1) to tenor (measure 5), to alto (measure 9), to soprano (measure 13). Fischer's six-note fugue subject has the same notes as Bach's (see example 69), but it is slightly, though importantly, different in rhythm. Fischer's subject starts with a whole note, speeds up to two half notes, but then steps backward to whole notes, which completely halts all forward progress. This inability to generate forward momentum will be one of the fundamental weaknesses of Fischer's fugue and offers a striking comparison to Bach's.

In a normal fugue exposition, each voice enters with the subject, either at the original pitch level, in which case it is still referred to as the subject, or transposed (normally up a fifth to the dominant), in which case it is referred to as the *answer*. (Some fugues never use any other versions of the subject than these two; others transpose the subject in the course of the fugue to different keys, producing a wider range of modulation. The fundamental listening principles do not change.) I mentioned at the opening of the chapter the importance of always asking, "What is fixed and what is free?" In a fugue, once a voice finishes with the subject, any other notes it might or might not play are up to the composer. In other words, the bass line, once it has finished the subject (in this example, on the downbeat of measure 5), is free to continue with any notes the composer likes. This is where counterpoint, the ability to compose interesting and independent voices, enters the picture and where Fischer fails so miserably. He shortens the first entry note in the tenor to a half note (measure 5), and the piece begins to pick up some rhythmic momentum. But then in measures 6 and 7 Fischer gives the bass nothing but two whole notes to accompany the tenor's subject, and the motion stops dead by measure 7. In fact, if you look at nothing but the combined rhythm of all the parts from measures 8 through 23, every single measure (with the small exception of measure 11, which has one quarter note) has the identical basic rhythm of two half notes!

The clearest test of contrapuntal writing is to sing or listen to each part independent of the others. If the writing is good, each part should be interesting by itself in addition to combining well with the other parts. Unfortunately, the voices that accompany the subject in Fischer's fugue could not be less interesting, as you can easily hear by following out the bass part after it finishes its subject from measures 6 through 14, and the tenor part after it finishes its subject from measures 10 through 13. Not only are these free voices uninteresting in and of themselves, they also do not change the sound of the subject in any significant way. They add no new dimension to our understanding of the subject's character. Even when Fischer uses his one contrapuntal device—stretto—it produces almost no effect.

A stretto is really just a round (like "Row, Row, Row Your Boat") on a fugue subject. In a stretto, one voice enters with the subject before the previous entry has finished. In Fischer's fugue, the soprano entry in measure 13 begins a three-part stretto. The bass enters in measure 15 before the soprano has finished, and the tenor enters in measure 17 before the bass has finished. The idea behind a stretto is to literally create the many out of the one: to make the accompaniments to a subject out of the subject itself. Yet Fischer's stretto sounds no different from any of the previous versions of the subject. The rhythm, harmony, texture, and shape change in no significant way. The stretto tells us nothing new about the subject, and by the time the passage finishes and cadences in measure 23, we have learned as much as we are going to learn and could easily end the fugue.

Bach's Fugue

EXAMPLE 69

Comparing Fischer's fugue with even a small portion of Bach's E Major Fugue from Book II of *The Well-Tempered Clavier* shows what composing and listening to fugue is all about. Like Fischer, Bach has the voices enter moving upward from bass to soprano in a subject-answer-subject-answer pattern. Except for the fact that Bach adds a short codetta to his exposition (with a superb section-ending cadence in measures 7 and 8), the external structure of the two expositions is essentially the same. Everything else, however, could not be more different. (A reminder once again that it is the measure-by-measure experience of a form that matters, not its structural diagram.) Even the small differences between the rhythm of Bach's and Fischer's fugue subjects are part of the two composers' different concepts of rhythm and phrase. We saw how Fischer's subject started with a whole note, sped up to two half notes, but then stepped back to whole notes, completely halting the subject's forward progress. Bach's subject also starts with a whole note and speeds up to half notes but then stays with half notes and continues to speed up further to quarter notes and eighth notes as the bass becomes a free voice in measure 2.

If counterpoint is all about singable, independent lines, merely comparing what Fischer's bass plays to accompany the tenor entrance in measures 5 through 7, with what Bach's bass plays to accompany the tenor entrance in measures 2 and 3 is a miniature master class in the art of counterpoint. Not only is Bach's bass line a superb melody in and of itself, with its own independent shape and rhythm, but its quarter-note pulse also utterly changes the meaning and sound of the subject, whose half-note pulse now ethereally floats above this active accompaniment. This accompaniment is as interesting and important for the listener as the fugue subject, and the bass line's core seven notes (motive *x*—the first six beats of measure 3) transposed in the tenor become the accompaniment to the alto entrance (measure 4) as well as the alto accompaniment to the soprano entrance (measure 6). When an accompaniment to a fugue subject returns along with the subject on a regular basis it is called a *countersubject*, and this countersubject is actually only one of three in the fugue. Yet even when one voice is playing the subject and another is playing the countersubject, Bach still has two free voices to add to the mix, and if you follow out each of the four independent voices, you will quickly get a sense of what contrapuntal mastery is all about.

As I mentioned at the opening of this discussion, the real interest for both the composer and the listener in a fugue is not simply the continual return of the subject itself, but rather the constantly changing musical contexts in which it returns. Each new accompaniment or countersubject changes the harmony and the meaning of the subject and allows us to hear it from a different perspective. As Schoenberg put it, Bach was a master at "creating the whole from a single kernel." Putting three small slices of this fugue next to each other for comparison will illustrate the principle in microcosm. In each of the three examples, the subject (E–F♯–A–G♯–F♯–E) is at the original pitch level, starting on an E.

EXAMPLE 70A

EXAMPLE 70B

EXAMPLE 70C

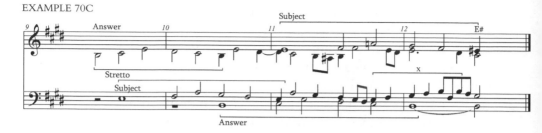

The first slice is the unaccompanied subject as it appears at the opening of the fugue. At this point, the subject is pure potential: a kernel and nothing more. We have no concept of how it will be harmonized, and it has a stately, almost solemn feel due to its limited melodic range and slow half-note pulse. The second slice is the alto entry just two measures later, accompanied by a free voice in the bass and the countersubject in the tenor. Already the development is staggering. The beautiful suspensions underneath the first and second notes of the subject, and the faster rhythm, noble rising scale, and climactic eighth-note snap of the countersubject have given this simple subject enormous depth by the fourth measure of the piece. Within seconds Bach has transformed our understanding of this subject more than Fischer does in his entire fugue.

The third slice shows what Bach can do with stretto. Unlike Fischer, Bach uses all four voices. The alto enters first, followed by the tenor, then the bass, and finally the soprano. The stretto builds magically from a single note to rich, four-part harmony and reshapes our understanding of the subject instant by instant. When in measure 12 the final note of the soprano line changes from the expected E to an E♯, the harmonic shock is stunning and leaves the world of Fischer's fugue behind forever.

Were we to look at all six strettos in this fugue, we would discover that every one shows the subject from a different angle, with different stretto combinations, different free voices, and different arrangements of old and new material. Though this entire fugue is constructed on a single six-note subject, that constraint for Bach is a source of strength. Focusing on a single subject is the way Bach frees himself "of the chains that shackle the spirit." The greater the limitations, the greater the freedom. The narrower the lens, the wider the view. Fugue, passacaglia, and chaconne force composers and listeners to look deeply at the possibilities contained in one bass line, one set of harmonies, or one fugue subject. They ask us to see the whole in a kernel; the many hidden in the one.

[12]

How Could This Come from That?

The Art of Theme and Variations

Pick up a ballpoint pen. Take off the cap and ask: "Is this still a ballpoint pen?" Yes, of course—albeit one without a cap. Unscrew the top part of the casing, remove the ink refill, and screw the top on again. Is that a ballpoint pen? Well, yes, just about. Is the refill a ballpoint pen? No, it's just the refill—but at least it can function as a pen, unlike the empty casing. Take the two halves of the casing apart. Is either of them a ballpoint pen? No, definitely not. No way. What happens to the thing as you dismantle it? When do the components cease (or start) to become a pen?

—ZEN EXERCISE, STEPHEN BATCHELOR,
BUDDHISM WITHOUT BELIEFS

What happens when you dismantle a theme? At what point is it no longer the theme? What component parts of a theme must a variation retain for it to be a variation? As we saw in chapter 11, when looking at variations of any kind, the fundamental question is always, "What stays the same, and what is changed? What is fixed and what is free?" In the forms we looked at in chapter 11, the answers to these questions were relatively straightforward. In a passacaglia, a recurring bass line stays fixed. In a chaconne, a recurring series of harmonies. In a fugue, a single-line fugue subject. In a theme-and-variations movement, however, the question of what is fixed and what is free is far more complex and forces us to grapple not only with the fundamental question of what constitutes a variation but also with the question of what constitutes a theme.

A quick word on history and terminology. Variations are traditionally divided into two categories. Passacaglias and chaconnes are called *continuous variations* because their variations follow each other without interruption. Theme-and-variations movements are called *sectional variations* because clear pauses at the end of the theme and each variation divide the piece into sections. Theme and variations can be complete, independent pieces, like Beethoven's *Diabelli Variations*, or they can be single movements in multimovement pieces, like the first movement of Mozart's Piano Sonata in A Major, K. 300. Variation is one of the oldest of all musical forms, and actual sets of variations have been composed in virtually every period of music from the sixteenth century to the present.

In order to understand theme and variations, we first need to consider carefully what we mean by the term *theme*. When we use the word casually, we tend to think of a theme as a melody or a tune, but for the purposes of a theme-and-variations movement, the word refers to every dimension and parameter that makes up the theme. A theme is its harmony, its bass line, its rhythm, its tempo, its key, its phrase structure, its length, its dynamics, and its texture as well as its melody, and any of these parameters may or may not be varied during the course of the piece. On the most simplistic level, if a variation were to change every one of these parameters, it wouldn't be a variation at all, just a new piece of music, while if it were to change none of these parameters it would be a literal repeat. Theme-and-variations movements operate in between these two end points: changing some aspects of the theme while keeping others intact. At their best, as simple themes generate extraordinary variations, the listener is left to wonder, "How could this come from that?"

A French "Twinkle, Twinkle Little Star"

Since the melody is the most easily recognizable feature of a theme, it is probably the element that is most commonly varied. Looking closely at one simple *ornamental variation* (the term derives from the fact that the melody is "ornamented") will allow us to quickly get at the listening principles behind hundreds of similar variations.

EXAMPLE 71

[continued]

EXAMPLE 71 [continued]

Though today we know the theme of Mozart's variations as "Twinkle, Twinkle Little Star," he knew it as a French song, "Ah! Vous dirai-je, Maman." The ABA, minuet structure of Mozart's theme is identical to the structure of "Twinkle, Twinkle Little Star" (see chapter 6), except that Mozart adds repeats to each half of the song, turning it into a classic two-repeat theme—the commonest form for variation themes. (There are fascinating, small differences in the two melodies, but they are not significant for the purposes of our theme-and-variations discussion.) The simple but elegant bass line matches the quarter-note rhythms of the melody but marks the three cadence points in the tune with half notes. (Notice the lovely way the left hand "joins" the melody for one brief moment at measures 15 and 16 to mark the middle cadence and prepare for the return of the opening.) The phrase structure could not be clearer: eight bars A, eight bars B, eight bars A. This is an archetypal theme-and-variations theme.

What Is a Variation?

Though it probably would be obvious to almost any listener on hearing this first variation that Mozart is simply decorating, or ornamenting, the melody, I would like to look closely at how he does it in order to establish basic listening principles that will apply to far more complex variations as well. Remembering that in variations the question is always "What stays the same and what changes?" it is clear that in this variation many things remain the same. The overall two-repeat, ABA structure stays fixed, along with the number of measures, the key, the dynamics, and the harmony. The bass line is virtually unchanged, though we will discuss the tiny alterations in measures 4 through 6 and measure 8 in the context of the melody later. The reason, of course, that so many things stay the same is so the listener can focus on the one thing that is different—the melody. What does it mean to vary a melody?

Think of each of the first four melody notes—C, C, G, and G—as anchor points. Since the tempo is moderate, there is space between each melody note to add other faster decorative notes. As long as these decorations pass through the melody's anchor points, we can hear the decorations as a variation on the original. The more times the decorations "hit" the anchor notes, and the more rhythmically emphasized these hits are (in a group of four sixteenth notes, the descending order of strength is first, third, second, and fourth), the clearer the connection to the original. For demonstration purposes, though this would be aesthetically intolerable, the clearest connection between decoration and original would simply be to repeat the anchor notes on every sixteenth note (example 72A). Still keeping all the hits on strong beats but cutting their number in half from four to two, we might decorate each note mindlessly with the note above each anchor note (example 72B). Even with only two hits per anchor, the connection to the theme is still clear. But if a composer decided that since each original melody note was repeated, all that was necessary to establish a connection to the original was one hit per measure—one C and one G—the connection would start to be more difficult to hear (example 72C).

EXAMPLE 72A   EXAMPLE 72B   EXAMPLE 72C

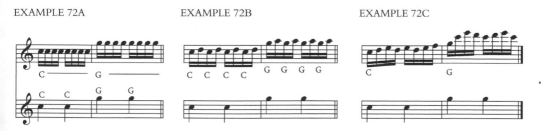

The simple point here is that the more times the decorated version plays the anchor notes and the more strongly the decoration emphasizes these notes, the clearer the connection to the original melody. In some ornamental variations, many anchor notes are skipped entirely, with hits only on certain key notes, and this can make the connection even more difficult to hear. In Mozart's variation, the hits are frequent, and the original tune is clearly audible.

Decoration as Idea

One of the challenges for the composer of this kind of ornamental variation is to follow the contours of the original melody yet still create an interesting independent idea—a new plot element—out of the decoration itself. Mozart creates the idea for this first variation out of the simplest kind of decoration—a neighbor note. A neighbor note is simply a decorating note a step above or below the main note, and Mozart uses both to generate his idea. The first and third sixteenth notes in the first measure of the first variation (D and B) decorate the anchor note, C, with the note above it (D) and the note below it (B). The technical name for this four-note figure is a *turn*, because of the way the four notes "turn" around the main note, C. The fifth and sixth sixteenth notes (B and C) simply decorate C with its lower neighbor note. (Notice that the anchor notes fall on the weak second and fourth sixteenth notes making the figure more fluid and less "clunky" than the figure in example 72B.) These two decorations—the turn figure and the lower-neighbor-note figure—combine to become the idea for the entire variation. The "turn-plus-neighbor-note" decoration (T+NN) grows out of the tune, but it becomes an independent musical idea—a new plot element—as well.

As we have seen so often, this new idea is immediately established through repetition, as the turn-plus-neighbor-note figure decorates the next two melody notes as well (G and G in measure 2). What makes Mozart great, however, is what *doesn't* happen in measures 3 and 4. He could easily have continued with two more measures of turn-plus-neighbor-note decorations (example 73).

EXAMPLE 73

But instead, he creates the kind of wonderful, subtle plot surprise that is at the heart of ornamental variations like this one by using the scale of measure 3 (see example 71, variation 1, measure 3) to create a brand-new idea in measure 4—"sigh and scale" (S+S). (A two-note "sigh" plus a six-note scale.) Since the first three measures of the variation moved in such a small, constricted, melodic space, the new idea's "big" leap up and "long" scale down feel like a breath of fresh air. Remembering that the original theme at this point simply went down a scale—G–G–F–F–E–E–D—Mozart goes down the same scale using the new sigh-and-scale decoration each time (example 71, variation 1, measures 4 through 8). For the truly attentive listener, there are two final delicious plot twists. First, there is a tiny change in the rhythm of the left hand in measures 4, 5, and 6. Instead of even quarter notes, there is a witty pause after the first note of each measure, followed by a fast sixteenth note, and this change of rhythm highlights the "main event"—the new sigh-and-scale figure in the right hand. The final touch at the end of the A section is also rhythmic, as the right hand elegantly slows from continuous sixteenth notes to eighth notes to articulate the section-ending cadence. In this graceful variation, we always know where we are with respect to the theme in terms of both the note-by-note flow of the melody and the overall structure.

The Meaning of a Variation

The second half of the variation follows similar principles to the first half but there are two points worth mentioning, not only because they recur in many other variation movements, but because they are central to the meaning of this kind of variation. We have mentioned several times the idea from chapter 2 that certain beginnings let you know who they are right away, while others ask the listener to wait. You may remember that this variation started off with a catchy "turn-plus-neighbor-note" idea, which vanished from sight after one repetition as the "sigh-and-scale" figure took center stage. (Of course, when the first part is repeated, we hear the turn-plus-neighbor-note idea twice more, which not only reestablishes it in our ear but also gets us used to hearing it as a section-opening idea.) Going forward through the piece, when we come to the end of the first variation's A section, the sigh-and-scale figure surely seems to be this variation's main event, with turn plus neighbor note a distant second in importance.

However, the second half of the variation (see example 71) shows how dangerous expectations can be, and how delightful it is to be wrong. Suddenly, sigh and scale disappears from the scene, and the forgotten turn plus neighbor note returns (slightly varied) four times to decorate "Up above the world so high." Mozart easily could have repeated it four more times for "Like a diamond in the sky" (the original melody, you remember, simply repeats), but instead he varies the *variation*, inventing a new decoration in measure 13 that keeps the turn but surprisingly adds an arpeggio. The truly great listener will notice that not only is the decoration in the right hand changed (measures 13 through 15), but the left hand is changed as well. Mozart puts the quarter notes of measures 9 through 11 on top of each other as half-note chords, and the new sustained chords exquisitely highlight the new "turn plus arpeggio" idea (T+ARP). Mozart's elegant variation on a variation ushers in a repeat of the opening A section to symmetrically bookend the variation. Having seen how the opening idea turns out in the B section, we hear its return with new forward-backward appreciation and understanding.

Bass, Mode, Meter, and Harmony

I have gone through this one ornamental variation so painstakingly because its listening principles are relevant for so many other Classical-period theme-and-variations pieces. While Mozart's variation decorates the theme's melody, this same kind of decoration can be applied to a bass line as well. Perhaps the most famous example is Bach's *Goldberg Variations*, which systematically varies the bass line of its theme through thirty variations. Just looking at the first four measures of the theme's essential bass line and comparing it to the same four measures in two variations will show the principle clearly (see example 74). Each variation creates its own independent idea by using the theme's bass line as the first note and anchor of each gesture.

EXAMPLE 74

Though any aspect of a theme's makeup can be altered, changing certain parameters, like mode and meter, produces striking, clearly audible results. Example 75A, from Mozart's "Ah! Vous dirai-je, Maman" variations, shows the powerful effect of changing a theme's mode from a major key to a minor key, while example 75B shows the effect of changing its meter from two beats per measure to three beats per measure.

EXAMPLE 75A

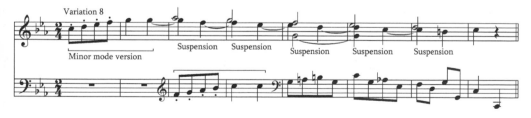

EXAMPLE 75B

As I mentioned at the beginning of this discussion, melodic decoration is a mainstay of theme-and-variations movements because the
tune is usually the most recognizable feature of a theme. However, a
theme (unlike a single-line fugue subject) includes its harmony, and
many composers keep the theme's harmony fixed while inventing
completely new melodies to go with it. When we remove the cap of
a pen it is still clearly a pen, but when we look at just its insides—the
refill—it can be difficult to recognize as a pen. Similarly, when a variation keeps only a theme's insides or harmony intact, the connection
between variation and theme can be difficult to hear. The challenge
becomes even greater when the variation does not duplicate the
theme's harmony identically but only incorporates its essential chords.
Examples 76A and 76B show this scenario using the first eight measures of the theme and the first eight measures of variation 10 from the
third movement of Mozart's Piano Sonata in D Major, K. 284

EXAMPLE 76A

EXAMPLE 76B

[continued]

EXAMPLE 76B [continued]

If you were to simply listen to these two phrases without knowing that they were part of a theme-and-variations movement, you might not even realize they were related. When we ask our standard theme-and-variations question, "What stays the same and what is changed?" it is the changes that are most immediately striking. The melodies of the two phrases bear almost no resemblance to each other, and the two textures could not be more unalike. The theme has a flowing right-hand melody and a smooth left-hand accompaniment, while the variation flips this basic arrangement upside down and puts a French-horn-like, left-hand melody underneath an oscillating, repeated note in the right hand. On first listening, only the number of measures, tempo, meter, and possibly the little melodic cadence figure in measure 4 seem to stay the same. However, closer listening reveals that the underlying harmony stays the same as well. Rather than duplicating the theme's original chords, Mozart instead keeps only the essential harmony unchanged. Using just the first two measures as an example, the theme originally had four chords: D, B minor, E minor, and A. The variation keeps only the essential harmony in each measure: the D chord and the A chord. Should the tenuous, overall connection between variation and theme cause any confusion, Mozart keeps the little cadential melody in measure 4 intact, so the listener can get his bearings, even if temporarily confused by the lack of a familiar melody or exact harmonic sequence.

The Beethoven Revolution

The composer who transformed the entire meaning of theme and variations was Beethoven. Early in his career, like other Classical-period composers, Beethoven wrote variations that were fundamentally ornamental. Though many of these pieces were highly accomplished, imaginative, and brilliantly virtuosic, they were essentially explorations of the external surfaces of his themes. In his middle- and late-period variations, however, Beethoven began to move away from this decorative, external approach toward a probing, internal search for essences. Like the Zen monk dismantling his pen, Beethoven began to dismantle his themes, piece by piece, stripping away their component parts, trying to get at their core, asking, "What happens to a theme as you dismantle it? When do the components cease (or start) to become a theme?" This new seriousness of purpose is evident even in the themes he chooses for his late-period variations, and the profundity and solemnity of the theme of his Piano Sonata op. 109 variations is light years away from the traditional Mozart/Haydn model.

EXAMPLE 77

Before Beethoven, theme and variations was not a fundamentally dramatic genre. These movements might be witty, charming, and elegant, and they might even contain isolated dramatic moments, but they were not structurally dramatic like sonata-form movements. Their drama was external, not internal: on the surface, not essential. Beethoven single-handedly elevated the seriousness and purpose of the genre and made his late-period variations movements profound journeys of discovery containing some of his most original and probing music. From the first notes of his op. 109 theme, it is evident that theme and variations has been shifted to a new spiritual plane. If beginnings are everything, this opening immediately creates a kind of timeless, otherworldly, spiritual universe before the variations have even begun.

Because Beethoven's approach to variation was so radically new, several of his late-period variation sets were not initially considered to be variations at all but instead were thought of as bundles of detached episodes. In fact, if you listen to the beginnings of variations 3, 4, and 5, with their drastic differences of tempo, texture, and mood, you might have no idea that they were related to the opening theme in any way.

EXAMPLE 78A

EXAMPLE 78B

EXAMPLE 78C

From Simple to Abstract

Beethoven's approach to variation in the piece ranges from simple to abstract. Some of the op. 109 variations are relatively traditional and use techniques we have discussed in this chapter. Variation 2, though completely altering the theme's tempo and texture, keeps its melody and bass line and decorates them both in familiar, if highly imaginative, fashion. Here are just the first two measures of variation 2, with the theme's melody and bass notes marked with asterisks.

EXAMPLE 79

If you go back and forth several times between these two measures in the theme and the variation, while paying attention to the asterisked notes, you can actually hear the variation as a decoration of the theme. Similarly, if you compare the first four measures of variation 3 (example 78A) with the first four measures of the theme, you can see that the left hand of the variation decorates the essential notes (marked with asterisks) of the theme's right-hand melody, while the variation's right hand plays the essential notes of the theme's left hand. Once you grasp this, it is easy to hear that the variation's next four measures simply switch hands.

Though this kind of variation is highly imaginative, it is not unrelated to the kinds of decoration we have already looked at in this chapter. What makes this piece, and Beethoven's entire approach to variation, unique is the abstract way he begins to conceive of his theme and the utterly new kind of connections this kind of abstraction makes possible. I will use just the first four measures of the theme and the first four measures of its second half to illustrate the point.

Abstract Hearing: How Could This Come from That?

If you listen to the first four measures of the theme from the point of view of harmony, you will hear basically three different chords in each measure, all connected by a smoothly rising bass line. What Beethoven does, taking Mozart's approach from example 76B to an extreme form, is to say that each of these four measures is essentially "about" one chord. Measure 1 in Beethoven's hearing is basically an E chord, measure 2 a B chord, measure 3 an E chord, and measure 4 a B chord. Forgetting all about the music's surface detail—shapely melodies, elegant chords, and fancy bass lines—for Beethoven, on the most basic level, the passage simply swings back and forth between two elementary chords, E and B. The two poles of the tonal universe: tonic and dominant.

What this means for Beethoven is that any four measures of music that use these four basic chords (E–B–E–B) are a variation on the theme. It is important to understand the truly radical implications of this simple statement and the bold new way of hearing it represents. It means that though the music of variation 4 (example 78B) has a completely different meter, tempo, texture, melody, accompaniment, bass line, and emotional feel than the theme, because the harmony of its four measures is fundamentally E–B–E–B, for Beethoven it is a variation. The music in the two passages is related. Once a theme is no longer its melody or its harmony but simply a kind of underlying essence, the possibilities for connection become almost infinite. Startlingly different kinds of music can suddenly seem to be profoundly related because on an elemental level they share the same fundamental harmonic common denominator.

Beethoven pushes this kind of abstract hearing even further in the second half of the theme. Remembering that a sequence is simply the repetition of a musical idea starting on a different note, the second half of the theme begins with a sequence in the melody and bass (marked x and y in example 77) followed by a move to a minor key in the fourth measure. What is astonishing is that in Beethoven's abstract way of hearing, these four measures are not meant to be understood as any aspect of their musical surface. Not their melody, their harmony, or their rhythm, but rather their essential concept: "a sequence and a move to minor." Once these measures are grasped as an underlying essence—"a sequence and a move to minor"—for Beethoven, any sequence and move to minor is a variation, no matter what the surface details of the music. All sequences and moves to minor are related. Suddenly, music like the four corresponding measures of variation 4 and variation 2 (examples 80A and 80B), which could not be more different in surface detail from each other and the original

theme, are related because they are all made up of a sequence and
move to minor.

EXAMPLE 80A

EXAMPLE 80B

This kind of abstract hearing, focusing on the essence of things
rather than their surface, is at the heart of the Beethoven revolution
not only in theme and variations but in other genres as well, and it
grows out of his obsession with connection. (This is why so often
pure similarity of rhythm connects seemingly unrelated ideas for
Beethoven. Rhythm as a fundamental component of a musical idea
acquires an unprecedented primacy in Beethoven's music, and
sketches of pure rhythm without pitch are frequent in his notebooks.)
Beethoven's compositional technique says, "We look at the surface of

things and see difference, yet the differences that separate us are super-ficial and illusory. What is fundamental is what is the same," and find-ing that fundamental connectedness and unity behind difference has become the work of the composition. It is a new purpose for theme and variations. Not simply to decorate a theme but rather to discover its core essence and create a universe out of that essence. "Only connect" wrote E. M. Forster. Beethoven's theme-and-variations movements show us how.

[13]

The Individual versus the Community
The Concerto

E pluribus unum [Out of many, one]

—THE GREAT SEAL OF THE UNITED STATES

In choosing which forms to discuss in this book, I have tried to pick ones that not only have a central place in the core classical-music repertoire but also contain a wide range of listening principles. I have divided these forms into two broad categories. Those based on contrast—thirty-two-bar song form, two-repeat minuet form, and sonata form—and those based on "one thing"—passacaglia, chaconne, fugue, and theme and variations. Since a comprehensive treatment of any of these forms, historically or theoretically, would go far beyond the scope of this book, I have instead tried to focus on essential listening principles: how each form works, and what is involved in experiencing that form. In certain cases, when a form has changed its meaning and purpose over time (as in the case of minuets, chaconnes, and passacaglias), I have tried to make some brief mention of these changes. Concerto, the final form I would like to discuss, has had almost completely different meanings and purposes at different points in time. A Baroque concerto by Vivaldi or Bach, a Classical concerto by Mozart or Beethoven, and a Romantic concerto by Felix Mendelssohn or Schumann represent three separate approaches to the relationship of soloist and orchestra, and each requires a unique way of listening. Without getting into extensive sketches or diagrams of concerto form, I would like to briefly discuss the fundamental differences in the way these three types of concertos function, and the variety of listening experiences they offer.

To Dispute or to Unite?

It is interesting that the two words at the center of the long-running, scholarly debate over the origins of the word *concerto* should reflect almost opposite approaches to the purpose of the form. Some scholars derive the word from the Latin word *concertare*, meaning "to contend or dispute," while others derive it from the common meaning of the Italian verb *concertare*, "to reach agreement, to unite." (There are also some scholars who suggest the Latin word *conserere*, "to join together," "to unite," as a source—see the *Harvard Dictionary of Music*—because the spelling *conserto* has sometimes been found.) Is the concerto fundamentally about the soloist and the orchestra "contending and disputing," or "reaching agreement, and uniting"? Though, as we shall see, there have been different answers to this question at different points in time, the history of the form is really the history of the many different ways composers have found to deal with, as the eminent music critic Sir Arnold Tovey put it, "opposed and unequal masses of instruments." Everything in a concerto grows out of the artistic challenge of handling two contrasting bodies of sound. In concertos from the Classical period on, this usually means a single soloist and an orchestra; however, in the Baroque period, concertos for several soloists, concerti grossi (grand concertos), were just as common as those for a single soloist (solo concertos). Both the concerto grosso and the solo concerto were "about" the deliberate contrast of two different sonorities: a group of solo instruments or a single solo instrument, and the mass of orchestral sound. If a concerto was written for several soloists (such as Vivaldi's many concertos for two violins and orchestra or Bach's *Brandenburg* Concerto no. 2 for trumpet, flute, oboe, violin, and orchestra) the solo group was referred to as the *concertino*. The orchestra as a whole was referred to either as the *ripieno* (full) or the *tutti* (all). How to make their contrast of sound expressive is the ongoing story of three hundred years of concerto writing.

Let's start getting a sense of basic concerto principles by looking at the Baroque version of the form.

One point I have tried to make throughout our discussion of forms is that in nearly all cases, form "recipes," with their accompanying diagrams and labels, were created after the fact by theorists trying to describe what composers had already done intuitively. Baroque concerto form did not exist as a fixed blueprint or set of rules in an eighteenth-century musical dictionary, but instead arose naturally over time as composers responded to recurring musical situations in ways that were imitated, varied, and developed from composer to composer and from piece to piece as the material demanded. The contrast between the two unequal masses of sound at the heart of the concerto—the soloist or soloists and the orchestra—is not simply a contrast of volume; it is also a contrast of expression. Finding a form that could make effective use of these differences of sound and expression is the essential challenge of the concerto, and a key element in that form, borrowed from the Baroque aria, is the ritornello.

The Ritornello

As Douglass Green puts it in *Form in Tonal Music*:

> A distinctive feature of the Baroque aria was the use of orchestral ritornellos. These passages, preceding, interrupting, and following the vocalist's part, act as contrast to it. There is an antiphonal give-and-take between two different bodies of sound: the full orchestra on the one hand, and on the other a soloist with a portion of the orchestra lending support. In the concerto a similar principle is at work except that both opposing bodies of sound are made up entirely of instruments. The forms that are associated with the concerto are a structural result of this opposition.

The opening orchestral ritornello is a key feature of the Baroque concerto, and its very first note instantly distinguishes it from all later versions of the form. (For the purposes of this chapter I am focusing on the most highly developed movement in the concerto—the opening movement. Once the essential solo-ensemble contrast has been established in the first movement, the forms of the second and third movements tend to be simpler, more direct, and less distinctive, and therefore require less explanation.) Here in full score is the opening fifteen-measure orchestral ritornello of Vivaldi's Concerto for Two Violins and Orchestra, op. 3, no. 8.

EXAMPLE 81

[continued]

EXAMPLE 81 [continued]

[continued]

EXAMPLE 81 [continued]

A simple way to think of the relationship between the soloist or soloists and the orchestra in a concerto is to think in terms of the relationship between individual and community. In a Baroque concerto, from the very first note, unlike in virtually every Classical-period concerto, the soloists play along with the orchestra. The importance of this simple fact cannot be overstated, since it goes far beyond structure to fundamental attitude and purpose. Though Baroque concertos celebrate individual expression and virtuosity, the individual remains a member of the community as a whole. Both solo violins play in unison with the ensemble violins throughout the opening ritornello with no compunctions about being "equals among equals." In fact, the one moment in Vivaldi's opening tutti where the soloists briefly play an individual solo role is a classic example of the exception proving the rule. In measures 4 and 5 the two solo violins play a tiny four-note figure (labeled *x*) in fast alternation with the violins of the orchestra. In a Classical, Romantic, or modern concerto, "throwing away" the soloist's first entrance on a quick, three-second passage of trade-offs would be almost inconceivable, but in a Baroque concerto, where the soloist is more intimately connected to the community, this spontaneous-sounding moment adds color and surprise to the tutti without in any way "demeaning" the soloists' importance.

Vivaldi's opening tutti is a classic example of a Baroque ritornello. It is entirely in the home key and it is made up of detachable parts: short, catchy ideas that can be easily rearranged, reordered, and excerpted for later use throughout the movement. Because the opening ritornello in a Baroque concerto, normally returns to end the entire movement, it frequently has a clear closing section and a final cadence like the section from measures 14 through 16, and this clear close returns several times in the movement. Any section of the opening tutti in a Baroque concerto can return in whole or in part during the movement, and a striking opening idea like Vivaldi's frequently returns as a structural marker transposed in various keys to guide the listener through the form. As in a Baroque aria, this opening orchestral ritornello, in whole or in part, ultimately precedes, interrupts, and follows the soloists' sections and continually acts as a contrast to them throughout the course of the movement.

The Solo Sections

The material in the solo sections of the piece shows how closely connected the worlds of the individual and the community are in the Baroque concerto and what a wide spectrum of musical relationships this intimacy makes possible. At one end of the spectrum, there are solo sections that feature the individual utterly separate from the community. In example 82, the entire orchestra drops out, leaving the two soloists to play completely alone. This short passage exhibits three fundamental listening pleasures of the Baroque concerto. First, the sheer delight in the sudden contrast of "opposed and unequal masses of instruments": the full orchestra playing *forte* versus the two unaccompanied soloists playing *piano*. The second pleasure is hearing the full-ensemble ritornello idea played and varied by a soloist or soloists with a completely different sound and texture (here, the thematic material the first solo violin is playing is the catchy, alternating solo/tutti idea from measures 4 and 5 that was such a surprise in the opening ritornello, now developed as a rising scale and recast texturally as a duet for two solo violins). This kind of transformation will occur in concertos of all periods. The third pleasure occurs at the end of the passage (measure 51), when the full orchestra bursts in *forte* with the movement's opening material (now in a new key) to finish the solo section. This quintessential concerto moment, as the piece's two unequal masses of sound dramatically confront, dovetail, and complete each other, almost defines the Baroque concerto.

EXAMPLE 82

Having the two soloists play alone with no accompaniment illustrates one extreme possibility for a solo section, but over the course of the movement Vivaldi offers a dazzling range of solo-ensemble combinations covering the complete individual/community spectrum. If the two soloists playing alone represent the extreme individual end of the spectrum, the next step toward community is to have a single group from the ensemble—just the bass instruments—accompany a solo section, as in example 83.

EXAMPLE 83

[continued]

EXAMPLE 83 [continued]

As I have said, the difference between the soloists and the orchestra is not just a difference of volume but also a difference of expression, and one way composers individuate their soloists is to give them their own musical material. From the individual/community perspective, it can be helpful for the listener to ask, "Is the material the soloists are playing shared community property from the ritornello or uniquely solo material?" The solo section in example 83 begins with the solo violin playing a sequential idea that has not previously been heard in the piece (Sequence 1). This kind of classic, concerto figuration almost defines "soloist music," and when the material is accompanied by nothing but the bass instruments and the harpsichord, the piece has momentarily found a new texture: Baroque chamber music. But there is more going on than just the appearance of a new and interesting texture.

The "chamber music" continues for four measures (measures 30 through 33) and then thins out even further to just cello and solo violin (measure 34). The violin's string-crossing pattern (marked *y*) is repeated and varied to end the solo section. But then, in a shocking individual/community moment, this quintessentially solo figuration suddenly becomes community property and is taken up and played in varied form by the entire orchestra.

It is important to understand what this sharing of material does and does not mean. It does not mean that in the Baroque concerto the worlds of the individual and the community are so seamlessly knit together that there is no room for individual virtuosity: that the soloists are no more than equals among equals. Anyone who has ever listened to Vivaldi's *Four Seasons* concertos or Bach's *Brandenburg* concertos knows the spectacular virtuosity that is possible in a Baroque concerto. What it does mean, however, is that though the community may celebrate gifted individuals and create opportunities for them to display their unique talents, these individuals are still part of the larger social fabric and capable of participating in the full spectrum of communal activities. They may play in unison with the tutti, they may share responsibility for copresenting ideas in conjunction with the tutti (x in measures 4 and 5), they may generate ideas that are later taken up by the tutti, or they may step forward as spectacularly virtuosic soloists with the rest of the ensemble in supporting roles. The most extreme form of this communal principle is Bach's *Brandenburg* Concerto no. 3, which is written for nine string players (three violins, three violas, and three cellos) in such a way that at various moments in the piece every single player becomes a soloist, part of a trio, and part of the complete ensemble. The piece represents perhaps the most perfect musical democracy ever created, and it reflects, in a sense, the ideal form of the Baroque concerto. Every individual gets to play every role the community has to offer, and each new combination of roles creates a new texture and a new sound. The possibilities are fluid and constantly changing, with roles and relationships continually being renegotiated. In Bach's universe and the universe of the Baroque concerto, there is room for it all.

Community in the Classical World

Ultimately, the form of each Baroque concerto grows out of the specific and varied ways its ritornello and solo sections alternate. There are no rules, formal requirements, or blueprints for how these movements are structured, though certain patterns in terms of the number of ritornello and solo sections, and the way their keys are organized, arise gradually over time. The overall shape of any individual concerto grows naturally and fluidly out of its particular material and narrative flow. As the Baroque world gave way to the Classical period, however, the forces that shaped sonata form (see chapter 10) began to affect the other forms of the period as well, and the concerto was no exception.

If you need a single image to grasp the essential difference between Baroque and Classical concertos—between a Vivaldi concerto and a Mozart concerto—you might well pick the opening note. As we saw in the Vivaldi op. 3 concerto, from the very first note, with rare exceptions, the soloists play along with the orchestra. The soloist, while special, is still a participating member in the community as a whole. He plays in unison with the tutti throughout the opening ritornello with no need to immediately assert "special status," and assumes a solo role only when the tutti drops out to reveal and accompany the already communally active soloist. In the Classical concerto, however, the soloist is "other"—separate from the community—from the very first note, and his absence throughout the entire opening tutti defines this otherness. Whatever else occurs in the opening ritornello, on the most fundamental level the listener is waiting for the entrance of the soloist—the dramatic entrance of an individual clearly separated from the group.

This clear distinction between the soloist and the orchestra— between individual and community—affects every aspect of the form, beginning with the single most recognizable feature of the classical period concerto: its so-called *double exposition*. The opening orchestral tutti in a Classical-period concerto, like its Baroque predecessor, stays entirely in the tonic key. However, in a Classical opening tutti (often called a *first exposition*), we are no longer dealing with detachable parts—short, catchy ideas that can be easily rearranged, reordered, and excerpted for later use throughout the movement. Instead the material is now shaped, paradoxically, like a sonata exposition that does not change keys. The opening tutti of Mozart's Piano Concerto no. 23 in A Major, K. 488, for example, is constructed exactly like a sonata-form exposition, with all of the "theme-establishing" passages, transitional passages, and passages of preparation we discussed in chapter 10 but without the all-important move to a second key that was an exposition's central harmonic event. Mozart's tutti opens with a theme that sounds exactly like the opening theme of a sonata-form movement (example 84A). Its second idea sounds exactly like a modulating transition section (example 84B). The cadence and pause at the end of the section sound exactly like the cadence and pause at the end of a sonata transition, and the theme that follows (example 84C) sounds exactly like a sonata-form second theme, yet we are still in the home key, and have transitioned nowhere. Creating an orchestral ritornello that has the shape and feel of a sonata-form exposition yet eliminates its most essential element—movement away from the home key—is the sleight-of-hand feat at the heart of every Classical-period opening tutti, and each particular concerto manages the feat in its own unique way.

EXAMPLE 84A

EXAMPLE 84B

EXAMPLE 84C

The opening orchestral tutti of the A Major Concerto, then, presents every element of a textbook sonata-form exposition: first theme, transition, second theme, closing theme, and coda, without ever leaving the home key. It is as if we are being given a preview of events to come, but with the crucial modulatory drama removed. Since in the Classical period, narrative drama is intimately connected to the movement away from the home key, an opening tutti that stays entirely in the home key, no matter how substantial it might be in length and complexity, will inevitably be introductory in nature. This of course is intentional, as the piece's principal dramatic actor, the soloist, has not yet entered the scene, and in a perfect blending of form and content, it is the soloist who initiates the central narrative move away from the home key.

We saw how closely related the worlds of individual and community are in the Baroque concerto and what a wide spectrum of musical possibilities this intimacy creates. In the Classical period, the worlds of individual and community are far more sharply differentiated, yet ironically this greater separation allows for a whole new relationship to evolve between soloist and orchestra that was unavailable in the Baroque concerto. In the opening ritornello, we are being introduced not only to the thematic material of the piece but also to the kind of musical expression the orchestra can make on its own. (Remember, the soloist plays no part in this tutti.) Take, for example, the first idea of Mozart's concerto. In the opening ritornello version (example 84A), its expression is distinctly "orchestral." The string-section theme is anchored by a steady quarter-note bass line in the first two measures. The second four measures start as a first-violin melody but quickly turn into a duet for first and second violins rising and falling in tandem. The phrase ends with a lovely orchestral detail as the cellos and basses gracefully echo the string cadence to lead to a repeat of the opening melody in woodwinds and horns.

Now compare this orchestral version carefully with the solo exposition's treatment of the same material (example 85). First notice how personal this opening melody becomes when the soloist plays it alone with fluid, left-hand eighth-note accompaniment instead of the steady quarter-note accompaniment of the opening. This is not just a contrast of orchestral sound versus solo sound; it is a contrast of expression as well—individual speech versus communal speech.

EXAMPLE 85

[continued]

EXAMPLE 85 [continued]

These first four measures immediately introduce us to the sound and expression of the unaccompanied soloist. As the passage continues, the orchestra gradually joins the soloist to create exquisite combinations and textures that neither could have generated on its own. First, the orchestra and soloist clearly divide responsibilities. The orchestra's lower strings take over the job of accompaniment, leaving the piano free to work with only the melody. But when the piano plays the orchestra's opening melody, it doesn't simply repeat its notes. Individual expression is inherently different from group expression, and the piano doesn't just repeat or decorate what the orchestra played, it rephrases it in its own language. The orchestra's eighth-note idea of measure 5 becomes a sixteenth-note idea in the piano's right hand in measure 71. The orchestra's violin duet of measure 6 becomes a right-hand/left-hand piano duet in measure 72. And the violins' rising scale in measure 7 becomes a glorious set of arpeggios in the piano in measure 73. The piano is not so much decorating the earlier orchestral version as it is translating it into its own language. The two passages are what I call "idiomatic equivalents," in which a full-ensemble idea is "translated" by a soloist into his own idiomatic speech—one of the glories of the Classical-period concerto.

The soloist is presenting this material in collaboration with the orchestra, and Mozart gradually introduces the new solo/ensemble sound world to the listener's ear as he did the orchestral sound of the opening tutti. Four measures establish the sound and texture of the solo piano. Then he adds only the lower strings as a bass line, with the piano playing nothing but the melody. The original trade-off between the upper and lower strings at the end of the melody (measure 8) now becomes a beautifully expressive trade-off between piano and violins (measure 74) to connect to the next new texture—full string section with breathtakingly beautiful, sustained string sound. When the strings enter in measure 75 to accompany the next portion of the melody, the piano is once again playing the first measure of the theme. When the piano first played these notes in measure 67, they were a translation of an orchestral theme into a solo-piano vocabulary. Now the exact same piano notes have a new orchestral texture underneath, and this retranslation of the material into piano/ensemble vocabulary generates new piano decorations and orchestral accompaniments as the phrase continues. The grammar and syntax of the piece are created moment by moment as the piano and orchestra work out the expressive possibilities of their combined vocabulary.

It is not just the separation of soloist and orchestra but also a deep compositional understanding and respect for what each group has to contribute to the total expression that creates the possibility of all of these new sounds, textures, and combinations. Having the orchestra simply accompany the soloist is merely one of many possible scenarios. There are just as many cases in which the primary expression is orchestral and the soloist accompanies or adds personal commentary to the orchestra. Though there are hundreds of routine passages in which continuous piano figuration accompanies core thematic material in the orchestra, here is a particularly subtle example from Mozart's second theme (see example 84C, measure 31). Though the melody in this version (example 86) is clearly orchestral in the first violins, the flute, and the bassoon, the decorating sixteenth notes in the piano add urgency and expression to the melody in a way that transforms and personalizes the emotion of the passage.

EXAMPLE 86

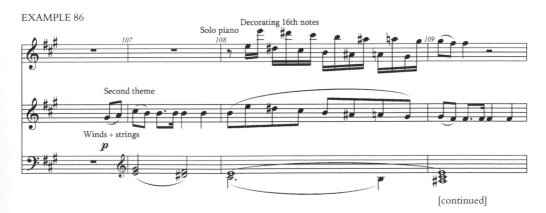

[continued]

EXAMPLE 86 [continued]

Once again we are reminded that form is a verb, not a noun. On a chart or a diagram, Mozart's piano exposition simply takes the material from the orchestral ritornello and replays it in sequential order as a second exposition for piano and orchestra while transposing the appropriate sections to a second key. However, looking closely at even a few measures has shown us how completely Mozart transforms his material melodically, orchestrally, and conceptually at every moment. The piano exposition translates the material of the orchestral tutti into a new combined solo/orchestral language in which almost anything is possible, including old material, translations and variations of old material, and completely new material. The piano exposition begins the harmonic motion and the true dramatic narrative of the piece not because any form description or recipe says so, but because the real drama of the movement starts when the concerto's two worlds join forces. From that point on, the piece is free to work out the sonata-form particulars of exposition, development, and recapitulation in joint solo/orchestral speech, making sure that in the end whatever is essential from both expositions is ultimately brought back and balanced.

The End of the Beginning or the Beginning of the End?

Let's quickly review the discussion to this point. In the Baroque concerto, the soloist, though clearly an individual, is also a part of the community. The enormous range of solo/ensemble combinations and textures Baroque concertos contain grows directly out of the intimacy of this individual-community relationship. In the Classical concerto, the worlds of community and individual are far more distinct, but both soloist and orchestra are vital, independent, expressive elements in a delicate balance between the individual and the community that is at the heart of the form.

R omantic composers like Mendelssohn and Schumann shattered this delicate balance, and their complete transformation of the form can be seen in the very first measures of Mendelssohn's G Minor Piano Concerto.

EXAMPLE 87

[continued]

EXAMPLE 88 [continued]

These twelve measures mark the end of the Classical concerto and the beginning of something new. The Baroque and Classical-period conception of an expressively, dramatically, structurally significant opening orchestral ritornello has been replaced by a ten-second orchestral "clearing of the throat" before the action begins. The seven measures of orchestral introduction have no expressive, dramatic, or structural significance whatsoever. They are the musical equivalent of, "On your marks—get ready—get set—GO!" and "GO!" refers to the soloist. Concertos like Mendelssohn's are "about" their soloist in a way that would have been unthinkable to Vivaldi or Mozart. A form based on the contrast of sounding bodies has become something completely different—a brilliant virtuoso display piece accompanied by orchestra. The concerto is no longer a world in which the individual and the community are intimately connected but instead a world dominated by a heroic individual. The orchestra has receded into a supporting role. Though the writing for orchestra may at times be quite elaborate, brilliant, and interesting, the importance of contrast between unequal masses of instruments has vanished as a structural principle. In a stunningly revealing choice, Schumann titled his cello concerto "Concertpiece for Violoncello with Orchestral Accompaniment." In the brave new world of the Romantic concerto, the soloist is king.

Finished versus Complete

Too many pieces of music finish too long after the end.

—IGOR STRAVINSKY

How do we know if something is finished? Is being finished different from being complete? The last movement of Haydn's *Joke* Quartet ends with a profoundly serious musical joke. Our very first example, in chapter 1, was a Haydn quartet that turned an ending into a beginning: the *Joke* Quartet is the exact opposite—a quartet that turns a beginning into an ending. The finale begins with a classic, lighthearted rondo tune.

EXAMPLE 88

[continued]

EXAMPLE 88 [continued]

The melody, harmony, and structure of this tune could not be clearer, and its treatment throughout the movement is conventional in every way. Every return is wittily prepared in standard rondo style, and all the returns of the theme occur exactly where we expect them to. Having heard the tune many times (the tune is actually the A section of an overall ‖:A:‖ ‖:BA:‖ rondo theme, so we hear these eight measures at both the beginning and the end of every return of the complete theme), we come to what seems like the final return, but its last note is followed by a disconcerting rest with a fermata over it (example 89, measures 141 through 148).

EXAMPLE 89

[continued]

EXAMPLE 89 [continued]

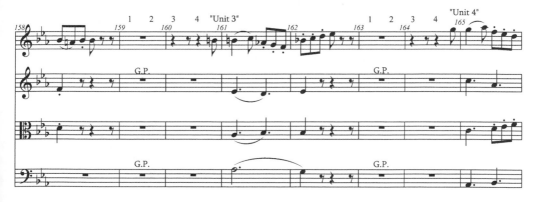

[continued]

EXAMPLE 89 [continued]

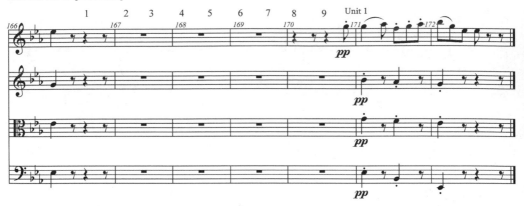

The pause in measure 148 makes us think, "Is that it? Is the piece over?" Though the phrase could technically be an ending—it is a perfect authentic cadence, and it is the ending of the rondo tune—it does not feel convincingly final in any way. The tempo then slows to adagio, and four strange, solemn measures are followed by another awkward rest with a fermata. Once again, this technically *could* be an ending, but it seems even less final. Why would Haydn end a quartet with four slow measures of brand-new music?

What happens next not only seems to explain everything, but explains it in a way that even audiences at the time would have thought of as "Haydnesque." The opening tune returns (measure 153), but with each two-measure unit followed by two measures of silence (essentially four "counts" of silence, as indicated on the score). By the time Haydn has gone through three of the four units we "get" the idea, so when the fourth and final unit finishes at measure 166, followed by extended silence, if the performers "play" the silence correctly (the visual element is crucial in this highly theatrical moment— a recording simply does not work), the audience should believe that the piece is finished. The moment is stunningly delicate. Though by all rights the piece is "done"—all four units of the main theme have been played, with intervening pauses—somehow things do not feel quite complete. Haydn clearly indicates that unlike the previous units, which were followed by four beats of silence, this last unit should be followed by *nine* beats of silence. Every instant of silence is filled with one screaming question: "Are we done?" And then after nine excruciating, wonderful beats of silence, Haydn adds two utterly extraordinary measures. To end the piece, just when the audience was beginning to accept that it had ended with the last two measures of the theme, Haydn repeats the opening two measures, *pianissimo*, and the beginning becomes an ending. However incomplete the piece felt with the last two measures of the theme as an ending, it cannot compare with how incomplete it feels with the first two measures as an ending. The listening gymnastics the audience must go through to truly hear the opening two measures as an ending are unprecedented. Haydn asks the listener to accept the incomplete as complete.

Definitions and Distinctions

The core definition of *finished* in the *Oxford English Dictionary* is "Brought to a conclusion, ended." This is the traditional, common-sense meaning of the word, as in "We finished eating" or "The symphony finished with a loud, full-orchestra chord." Something "finished" is done or ended.

Complete is defined as, "To make whole or entire, so as to leave nothing wanting." As in "Having finally seen the Acropolis, he could now say his life was complete."

This is the sense of the word that is at the heart of this chapter's central distinction between something that is finished and something that is complete. Between something that has simply ended, and something that has ended in a way that "leaves nothing wanting." "Finished" is a fact. "Complete" is a feeling, a state of mind. Haydn's *Joke* Quartet is finished, but it feels anything but complete. What makes a piece of music (or a book, a conversation, a relationship, or a phase of life) feel complete—whole and entire?

With the rare exception of a piece like the *Joke* Quartet, the terms *finished* and *complete* are largely interchangeable in the music of the Classical period. When a symphony of Mozart or Beethoven reaches its last measure with what is so often a formulaic, clear-cut, final cadence, it is invariably both finished and complete. Whatever tonal, thematic, and structural issues the piece has presented have been dealt with, and as in a detective novel, the compositional "case," so to speak, is closed. "Does this piece feel complete?" is a question to ask yourself at the end of every new work you hear. If a Classical-period piece is incomplete—if at the end it seems as if musical issues remain unresolved, or if thematic materials seem insufficiently explored—it is the result of poor composition, not intentional aesthetic choice. In the rational, Enlightenment world of the Classical period, finished *and* complete was the only acceptable aesthetic goal, and the *Joke* Quartet is the quintessential exception that proves the rule.

Romantically Incomplete: Schumann

In the Romantic period, however, this Classical-period world of clear contours, stable frames, and neatly tied up narratives is often replaced by a world of blurred edges and cryptic content, and some of the nineteenth-century's most profound and subtle revolutions have to do with this distinction of finished versus complete. In chapter 8 we discussed Schumann's "Träumerei" as if it were an independent, self-contained work, but it is actually the seventh number in a collection of thirteen short piano pieces called *Kinderszenen* (Scenes from Childhood). What makes so many of the individual miniatures in Schumann's collections of short character pieces (such as *Carnaval* and *Papillons*) magical is the way they are both complete in and of themselves, yet also incomplete, acquiring their full expression only when followed and preceded by the other numbers in the cycle. A great performer must manage this delicate balancing act of independence and dependence by playing each number as if it is both a finished, self-contained piece (independent) and also a fragment (dependent), needing to connect to the next number for true completion.

Many of the most beautiful examples of this blend of independence and dependence occur not only in Schumann's piano cycles but in his song cycles (also collections of complete yet incomplete fragments), in particular in the exquisite opening song of *Dichterliebe*, "Im wunderschönen Monat Mai" (example 90). This tiny, twenty-six-measure "fragment" subtly destroys the sanctity of the Classical frame at both ends. Though it is the opening of a sixteen-song cycle, the piece begins as if in mid-thought, as if the cycle had already begun. The piano prelude has the blurred texture of a dream memory, and its languid mood exists nowhere in the text of this uniformly happy poem about the "wonderful month of May."

EXAMPLE 90

[continued]

EXAMPLE 90 [continued]

In radical fashion, Schumann's piano introduction not only does not begin on a stable tonic chord in the key of the song, but it does not begin on the tonic chord of any key; it is not even clear what key we are in. The distinction between something that is finished and something that is complete can apply not only to an entire piece but to a single musical gesture or harmonic progression as well. The piano basically rocks back and forth between two chords (labeled 1 and 2 on the score), with the second chord being "The" of "The End." Grammatically the two chords "should" complete their gesture with an arrival on "End"—an F♯-minor chord—but the chord never arrives. It is suggested but never actually played. The piano prelude is "romantically incomplete."

Though the vocal entrance seems to clarify the key momentarily by resolving beautifully to a major chord on the words "*Monat Mai*" ("month of May"), after one repeat we leave the key of "May" behind and within moments find ourselves lost again, back to yearning, back at the original ambiguous piano introduction. Every gesture in the piece seems to be incomplete. The piano introduction suggests a key but never arrives; the vocal verse seems to clarify the key but immediately leaves it behind, and two more brief harmonic arrivals are also instantly undercut. The rapid succession of confusion/clarification/ more confusion is the fundamental way this piece moves, with each gesture finished but not complete. Like a Möbius strip, the song seems to make an endless loop that continually turns back on itself. The repeat of the piano introduction leads into the second verse, which is a repeat of the music of the first verse with new words. This in turn leads back to the piano introduction yet again; however, this time the song ends astonishingly on the introduction's concluding dominant-seventh chord.

A dominant-seventh chord is the virtual opposite of a final chord. It is a chord that is defined by its need for resolution. It is "The" of "The End," and ending a song on it is like ending a movie with The. . . . Though the next song begins with "End," the chord that the first song's final chord wants to resolve to, it is important as performer and listener not to make this simpler than it is. It is not that the first song is merely pausing on a dominant ("The") before connecting to its mate, the tonic ("End"); Schumann marks a long ritardando (slowing down) over the last three measures of the first song, and four different fermatas to make sure the final dominant-seventh chord is held and that we truly end the song on "The." It is essential to come to terms with the chord solely in the context of the first song and hear it as an ending that is complete in and of itself. Schumann in this subtle song is demanding that we completely rethink the most basic elements of our musical vocabulary. That we hear tonal music's most fundamental dissonance, its most unstable chord, as stable. The pianist must linger on that chord until we no longer hear it wanting to resolve, but instead, miraculously, hear it as resolved. We must reconfigure our listening in such a way that we can hear the incomplete as complete. Only when we have accepted this radical new entity—a dominant-seventh chord without need for resolution—can it then resolve, out of choice not need, in the "old" way (which now sounds new) into song two, "Aus meinen Tränen." Schumann's subtle yet revolutionary meditation on the difference between finished and complete emancipates dissonance (frees a dissonant chord from the *need* to resolve) in an intimate yet profoundly radical way.

Romantically Incomplete: Chopin

The poet Novalis said that the essence of Romanticism was "to make the familiar strange and the strange familiar," and that is the key to understanding Chopin's approach to completion in his revolutionary A Minor Prelude, which is equally radical yet diametrically opposed.

EXAMPLE 91

[continued]

EXAMPLE 91 [continued]

Chopin, like Schumann, attacks the clarity of the Classical frame from the very first measure, though in a completely different way, and with a completely different expressive result. Beginning a piece of music with a repeating accompaniment pattern (in the Broadway world called a *vamp*) followed by the entry of the melody is quite common, but here this standard procedure is grotesquely distorted. To use Novalis's language, every element in this opening contributes to making something "familiar"—a standard vamp-then-melody setup—"strange." First of all, the "vamp" is awkwardly low in the piano's range, and with two notes rather than three notes on each beat, the harmony is willfully obscure and dissonant. The very strangeness of this sonority *is* the aesthetic point, and the slow tempo (the slower the better) makes this strangeness even stranger. However, the key harmonic element in the opening, which is the key to the overall structure of the whole piece, is the fact that this "prelude in A minor" (which for Bach would mean beginning and ending on an A-minor chord) opens with a dirgelike accompaniment on the "wrong" chord: an E-minor chord.

Even more disconcerting is the fact that as the piece continues, no A-minor chord, cadence, or key is anywhere to be found. In addition, as in the Schumann song, the moment the music arrives in any key, it is immediately left behind. Finally, near the very end of the piece, after we have given up hope of ever finding A minor, or a stable key of any kind, the music clarifies its harmonic direction and begins to head toward a clear cadence in E. When three measures before the end Chopin finally gives us an absolutely crystal-clear, three-chord cadence—E–B–E ("The End")—we not only believe that the piece is over (or about to be over with perhaps one more decorated repeat of the cadence), we believe that we understand its plot in classic forward-backward fashion. The title (i.e., the key signature), we think, was somehow a mistake, and the piece is really a prelude in E minor. If this were the case, everything would make sense. The strange, opening "vamp" on E minor would have finally reached its goal with this final cadence on E major, completing a cryptic, but ultimately closed, circular journey from E minor to E major. Finished and complete. The performer must play the E-major chord two measures before the end as if it is, in fact, the chord the piece has been heading toward all along. As if the piece were a prelude in E, not A. (Remember from our discussion of forward-backward listening, thinking that the E chord is the goal of the piece and being wrong are both part of experiencing the piece.)

Then comes the astonishing moment. Just as we are sure the piece is finished and complete—a circular journey in the key of E—Chopin adds two more chords, which sound almost like an afterthought. However, these two chords are, in fact, "The End"—the quintessential final cadence of tonal music—in A minor! The piece is a prelude in A minor after all. The closing gesture and fundamental key of the piece, however, could not sound odder or more unprepared. If ever the familiar (tonal music's most basic cadence, "The End") was made strange, here it is. Though the piece has ended, it feels utterly incomplete, leaving us with nothing but questions. Like Schumann's song, it asks us to reevaluate the most basic elements of our musical vocabulary. What does it mean for a piece to be in a key? Can a piece be "in A minor" if nothing but the last two chords are in that key? (The musical equivalent of declaring a place you visit two days a year as your principal residence.) Can a key be a destination we reach utterly inconclusively, only at the end of a piece? Unlike the definitive endings of Classical-period pieces, fragments like Schumann's and Chopin's end with questions not answers and demand that we find a way to be complete with that.

Romantically Incomplete: Liszt

Both Schumann's song and Chopin's prelude are individual numbers in larger collections, and though they are provocatively incomplete, neither piece bears the responsibility of ending an entire work. However, there were nineteenth-century composers bold enough to experiment with inconclusive final endings as well, and two examples by Franz Liszt, cited by Charles Rosen in *The Romantic Generation*, expand the principles we have seen in Schumann's song and Chopin's prelude in thought-provoking ways. Example 92 is the ending of a solo piano piece of Liszt's entitled "Harmonies poétiques et religieuses."

EXAMPLE 92

At the beginning of the example, the piece seems to be heading toward a routine ending. The deception in measure 117 and the delay that follows are typical ways to strengthen a final cadence (see chapter 4 on cadence and delay), and by the end of measure 121 we seem to be about two measures away from finishing the piece in a reasonably normal way. (In addition to asking yourself, "Does this piece seem complete?" when it ends, it can be valuable to ask yourself, "Does this piece seem as if it is about to be complete?" as it nears its ending.) Then, all of a sudden, three measures before the end (marked lento disperato), everything falls apart. The tempo slows down drastically (lento), the expression becomes anguished (disperato), and the rhythm becomes spasmodic, jerking to a halt on a diminished-seventh chord in the penultimate measure. For non-musicians, a diminished-seventh chord is a close relative of the dominant-seventh chord that ended the Schumann song, and it is, if possible, even more fundamentally dissonant and unstable. (A series of diminished-seventh chords rising up the scale is the film composer's formula for creating "movie-music suspense.") After pausing on this intensely dissonant diminished-seventh chord in the penultimate measure, Liszt stunningly ends the piece by simply taking the melody notes of the lento disperato measures (marked x in the score) and playing them completely unaccompanied in the left hand at the bottom of the piano.

It is important to pay careful attention to how you listen to this final measure, since it is a radical extension of the listening required by the end of our Schumann song. The notes of the final measure are, as we have said, the same as the melody notes of the two preceding measures. The diminished-seventh chord that harmonized the melody in measures 122 and 123 is still ringing in our ears as the imagined "harmony" of the final unaccompanied measure when it begins. But as the seven last notes are played (the tempo marking is piu lento—even slower), we lose the memory of the chord, and the low bass notes start to sound independent of any accompaniment. If you listen very closely, in spite of the fact that these seven notes are theoretically still under the sway of our diminished-seventh chord, by the last note (E-flat) there is a sense of resolution, as if E-flat, the final note, has become a strange, momentary resting place. As with our Schumann song, the pianist must linger on this final E-flat until we no longer hear it wanting to resolve, but instead hear it as resolved.

Once again, we must reconfigure our listening in such a way that we can hear the incomplete as complete.

The Need for Closure

All of these experiments with inconclusive endings and incomplete forms can be disconcerting to listen to, as they go against our deeply felt desire for closure. In a revealing example of just how provocative and unsettling these kinds of endings can be, Charles Rosen cites Liszt's song setting of Victor Hugo's "S'il est un charmant gazon." The original 1844 version of the piece had a radical piano postlude that ended the song without resolution of any kind (see example 93). One can only assume that this inconclusive ending disturbed performers and audiences alike, since the published version from 1860 adds two utterly conventional extra measures, marked "ad lib," for pianists (and audiences) who could not tolerate the incompleteness and wanted more conventional closure.

EXAMPLE 93

As Liszt's optional ending makes clear, the desire for completion and resolution is a powerful one, and there is something immensely satisfying about a piece of music that manages to conclude with all its loose ends neatly and elegantly tied up. Perhaps because it is so rare in life, we value works of art that realize the full potential of their ideas and are both finished and complete. However, unsettling works that redefine completion, like the pieces discussed in this chapter, offer important and valuable lessons. Each of these pieces takes music that at first hearing appears incomplete and declares it to be complete: whole and entire, leaving nothing wanting. Works like these challenge the very idea of neatly tied up narratives with their illusory certainty and resolution. In his profound essay *Circles*, Emerson said, "People wish to be settled; only as far as they are unsettled is there any hope for them." Schumann, Chopin, and Liszt offer music for the "unsettled" listener with a radically new sense of completion. Like the Impressionist painters who exhibited as "finished" paintings that their contemporaries saw as incomplete sketches, these composers define completion on their own terms. Their music says, in essence, "Though this might not sound or feel complete to you, I declare it complete." A new vocabulary of hearing is asserted by a compositional act of will.

Is the *Unfinished Symphony* Unfinished?

If something can be finished yet incomplete, what about the opposite? Can something be unfinished yet complete? Throughout his career, Schubert left an enormous number of compositions unfinished, but none has become as well known as his *Unfinished Symphony*. The piece, composed in 1822, was clearly designed to be a standard four-movement symphony. There are sketches and an orchestrated fragment of a third movement, and empty score pages for what would have been a fourth movement; however, for reasons that remain unknown, only the first two movements were finished. Though many attempts have been made to complete the work, it is almost always performed "incomplete" in its two-movement form. Both of these finished movements are exquisitely lyrical, and they have a personal, intimate quality unlike those of any other symphony. The sketches for the third-movement scherzo come from a completely different expressive world and try unsuccessfully to bring the piece back into a more traditional, objective, symphonic mold. Though we can never know for sure why Schubert left the work unfinished, perhaps having made these sketches he realized that the first two extraordinary movements had already said all that he wanted to say in this vein. Perhaps for him the work was *unfinished* (not a full four-movement symphony) but *complete*, if not in a traditional way.

However, even if this was not Schubert's intention at all, and he simply left the work unfinished for practical reasons, fully intending to finish it at a later date, *we* can still decide for ourselves that it is complete. When we come to the end of the second movement, like Schubert, we have a choice. We can decide that the two movements are "whole and entire, with nothing lacking." Or we can hear them as an incomplete torso. An unfinished symphony. It is ultimately up to us to decide whether the *Unfinished Symphony* is unfinished.

Finished yet Incomplete

If a symphony can be unfinished yet complete, it is my sincerest hope that this book will be finished yet incomplete. That it will be a beginning, not an ending—a point of entry to the topics discussed in each chapter and to the approach to listening they contain. My wish is not simply that you hear the music in this book more perceptively and fully, but that you begin to hear all of the music that is *not* in this book in the same vital, active, participatory way. What counts is what happens once you put the book down. As Copland said, "No composer believes that there are any short cuts to the better appreciation of music. The only thing that one can do for the listener is to point out what actually exists in the music itself. . . ." The listener must do the rest." Measure by measure. Movement by movement. Piece by piece.

All you have to do is listen.

[POSTLUDE]

The Role of the Performer

In 1950 Roger Sessions wrote a wonderful book called *The Musical Experience of Composer, Performer, Listener.* Without the participation of all three partners in this triangle, no musical experience is complete, and having focused on the composer and the listener throughout this book I would like briefly to discuss the impact of the performer. Up until now, we have been proceeding as if a piece of music is the notes printed in the score. But a listener sitting in a concert hall is not actually hearing Beethoven's *Pathétique* Sonata, but rather a particular pianist's interpretation of it. Looking closely at the meaning and implications of this seemingly obvious sentence will be the focus of this chapter. What is interpretation, and how does the interpreter affect the composer-performer-listener exchange? To begin to understand interpretation and its impact on listening, we must first examine some of our most basic assumptions about what a piece of music is and how musical notation works.

Written Words/Written Music

Conceiving of a piece of music as the notes printed in the score seems at first glance to be a reasonable approach. Unlike some forms of

music that are largely improvisatory, Western classical music is fundamentally a written-down art form. Whether we hear a symphony in
our head while reading from the score, or listen to a live or recorded
performance, a printed score is the basis for the sound. Though this
might lead us to think of a piece of music as something stable and
permanent contained within the notes of a printed score, on closer
inspection this solidity turns out to be illusory. A quick look at the
difference between the spoken and the written word can provide a
useful frame of reference.

The Written Word

In *Understanding Media*, Marshall McLuhan discusses a famous acting
exercise in which the great theater director "Stanislavsky used to ask
his young actors to pronounce and stress the word 'tonight' fifty different ways while the audience wrote down the different shades of
feeling and meaning expressed." Though an actor may be able to
express fifty different shades of feeling and meaning using tone, pitch,
volume, accentuation, and facial and body gestures when he says
the word out loud, the written word for all of them is the same—
t-o-n-i-g-h-t. As McLuhan points out, the written word takes this rich
web of dramatic meaning, removes its aural subtleties and nuances,
and abstracts it into a single, cool, visual, symbolic representation—the
phonetic word. Though we casually consider the written and spoken
forms of the word to be identical twins, they are really distant
cousins. If the written word wants to convey all the rich meanings
contained in the spoken version, it must spell them out one by one.

But writing does more than remove the spoken word from its rich
web of audible, nuanced meanings. In addition, the written word
physically removes the writer and the reader from each other. Historically speaking, it shifted the relationship from a social context of intimate connection to one of separation—from a tribal culture, in which
communication meant speaking directly in each other's physical
presence, with facial expressions and gestures as part of the communication, to a literate society, in which the individual in isolation
"translates" his thoughts into abstract visual representation—words—
and has them sent to a recipient who reads the words in isolation and
then "retranslates" their meaning.

Written Music

This distinction between speaking and writing, and the shift from the world of the "tribe" to the world of the isolated individual, is also at the core of the history of notated music. Early civilizations almost never wrote down their music. The transmission was oral—within the tribe, from singer to singer—with the first notational systems simply serving as an aid to memory. A composer in the modern sense of the word didn't really exist at all. Since music was passed from person to person in oral fashion with both parties present, it was easy to transfer the music with all of its nuances and subtleties intact. The elder, priest, or teacher sang. The novice, chorus, or congregation imitated. However, the moment there was a desire or need to communicate a chant or a piece of music to someone not physically present, the whole situation changed. Some medium was needed that could represent the piece, and this was the real beginning of notation. What is absolutely crucial to understand here is that musical notation is not the music itself, but rather a metaphor, like the written word, in the dictionary's sense of "a symbol in which one thing is used or considered to represent another."

Metaphor

When Stanislavsky's actors said the word *tonight*, they were capable of pronouncing it expectantly, breathlessly, scarily, hopefully, and so on. But the written word is an abstract skeleton that represents or "stands in" for the richly nuanced oral version. It is not the same thing. It is a metaphor.

Similarly, there are just as many ways for a singer to sing the written pitch C as there are for Stanislavsky's students to say the word *tonight*. But though this sung C might also have fifty different shades of feeling and meaning, the written note ignores this, leaving in their place a circle on a piece of music paper:

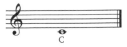

An abstract skeleton that represents or "stands in" for the richly nuanced, sung version. A metaphor.

Our present-day musical notation system, developed over hundreds of years, is in certain respects a far richer symbol system than that of the alphabet. In terms of notational symbols, there are only a handful of ways you can alter a written word to suggest different oral nuances. You can boldface, italicize, or underline a word, or you can punctuate it with a question mark or an exclamation point. But these symbols are crude compared to the oral subtleties they are trying to depict. They are metaphors—"symbols in which one thing [e.g., boldface type or an exclamation point] is used to represent another" (vocal emphasis).

Music, with its enormous aural range, has a far wider assortment of notational possibilities. There are ways to indicate the relative softness or loudness of a note with fine gradations in between: *pppp*, extremely soft, to *ffff*, extremely loud, with *ppp, pp, p, mf, f, ff,* and *fff* in between. There are several kinds of accents

a range of articulations from short notes with instantaneous release to broad sustained notes

connections between notes, gradual increase or decrease of volume over the course of a phrase

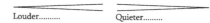

Louder.........   Quieter.........

and even indications with a precise metronome mark as to how fast or slow to play a phrase. (Think of how wide the tempo possibilities are in speech. How many different speeds you might use to say, "To be or not to be, that is the question." Imagine Shakespeare trying to find the right metronome mark to indicate how fast the speech should go and where it should speed up and slow down.) There is also a whole repertoire of printed words available to describe, in doubly metaphorical fashion, everything from the simple, basic character of a piece—

"lively," "fast," "*energico*," et cetera—to poetic, atmospheric descriptions like the Debussy marking we looked at earlier: "*Ce rhythme doit avoir la valeur sonore d'un fond de paysage triste et glace*" (This rhythm must have the sonorous value of a melancholy and frozen landscape).

But despite all these varied possibilities, just as the written alphabet represents in impoverished form the spoken word, musical notation represents in impoverished form sung or played music. Every composer understands this the moment he begins to write down an idea. No matter how fluid and competent you become at the painstaking, time-consuming, analytical, and highly conscious process of translating what you have just improvised at the keyboard into written notation, you cannot help but be aware how different it is from the played music with all its living accents, contours, dynamic variations, and subtleties of touch, phrasing, and tempo. Every playwright who has attended a rehearsal of one of his plays knows how incapable the written word is of conveying the multidimensional vibrancy of the spoken word, and every composer who has attended a rehearsal of one of his pieces knows how incapable written music is of conveying the multidimensional vibrancy of played music.

The parallel between written music and written words extends to the social dimension as well. In the same way that the written word physically separates the writer and the reader from each other, musical notation eliminates the need for the composer and performer to be in each other's presence. Once the composer has translated his music into its abstract visual form, his notes—his metaphors—can travel in his place, to be read by performers who "retranslate" these notes back into living music for the listener. On the one hand, this allows a composer's music to reach an almost unlimited number of people. However, it puts the fate of this music almost exclusively in the hands of its "retranslators." If the printed score is a metaphorical skeleton, it is up to each performer to decide how to put flesh back on its bones. To decide what "lively," "crescendo," "*pianissimo*," and "lightly" should sound like. To choose how each phrase should be shaped, what nuances to bring out, what notes to emphasize, and how the various elements and instruments should be balanced, and make all of the thousand other decisions that can never be put down in writing. Each performer of the *Pathétique* Sonata takes Beethoven's metaphorical blueprint and breaths life into it in his own unique way, creating an evanescent, one-time-only version that exists solely while the performance is occurring. Though a piece of music may seem to be something fixed, in actuality, it is more like a Tibetan sand painting that is continually created and destroyed, one unique, impermanent performance at a time.

Recorded Music

The invention of recorded music transformed every aspect of the composer-performer-listener relationship. The impact of recordings on the history of music has been as revolutionary as the invention of notation. At the heart of the revolution is the ability of a recording, for the first time in history, to make the impermanent, permanent. To have a single performance live forever.

A gifted musician has a lifelong, ever-changing relationship to a piece that evolves and changes with repeated performances. Each individual performance is a commitment only to one's understanding of the work at that moment in time, in that particular hall, with that particular audience and group of performers. No pianist's performance of Beethoven's *Appassionata* Sonata is a final, definitive, for-all-time version, until it is captured and frozen on a disc.

A set of possibilities becomes a fixed interpretation, and an ephemeral performance becomes a physical commodity. We have already seen that musical notation allowed composers to communicate with performers without having to be physically present, thereby vastly expanding the reach of their art. Performers, however, still had to appear in person and could only reach those they could physically play for. Recordings, however, did for performers what notation had done for composers—allowed them to communicate their message with no human contact required. For the first time in history, performers could reach listeners (via record, tape, CD, or broadcast) without having to be physically present. Every rung on the composer-performer-listener ladder could now exist in isolation. If the classic nineteenth-century visual depiction of a musical listener is a painting of a "family musicale," a salon performance, or a concert, the quintessential twenty-first-century visual image is an individual walking down the street with iPod headphones in his ears, utterly isolated, oblivious to everything and everyone surrounding him. To use McLuhanesque terminology, isolation and separation have become unintended consequences of the medium of recorded music.

The physical separation of the performer and the listener is not the only separation produced by recorded music. Until the invention of recorded sound, a piece of music was nearly always connected to a function and a space. Different kinds of music were created to accompany a church service, celebrate a king's birthday, showcase a virtuoso, or provide domestic entertainment; and music for a mass heard in a church, dance music played outdoors on a royal barge, a concerto heard in a concert hall, and a string quartet played at home in a "chamber" were all created with those specific acoustical spaces in mind. Recordings, however, eliminate any connection to function, occasion, or performing space (completing a process begun in the concert hall) and place all music, whether a twelfth-century trouba-dour song, a Gregorian chant, a Wagner opera, or an electronic tape collage, in the same eerie, cool, neutral, electronic space generated by the medium's speakers. Music as a concrete human activity rooted in function and space becomes pure sound, divested of circumstance and location, heard in isolation.

The invention of recorded sound, of course, has had an enormous upside as well. It has not only vastly expanded listening, but it has democratized it as well. Music and performers that for hundreds of years had been available essentially to only a small, privileged segment of society in a few cultural centers became available to nearly every-one, nearly everywhere. Geography became virtually irrelevant, as great performers and composers were able to communicate their artistry to millions of listeners worldwide whom they otherwise never could have reached. In the same way that printing ultimately made the literary canon universally available, recordings made the classical-music canon (the "standard repertoire") universally available. Music that had once been hearable perhaps once in a lifetime only on the king's barge or at the emperor's court could now be heard by anyone, anywhere, at any time merely by pressing Play. Suddenly everyone was welcome at what had for centuries been an elite, members-only, private party. Composer, performer, and listener might never meet in person, but through the magic of recording technology their exchange became available to all.

A Message in a Bottle

In the end, printed music initiates a dialogue that is both poignant and life-affirming. An isolated composer, in the hope of communicating and connecting, turns living, breathing music into a metaphor and sends off a musical score, like a message in a bottle, to an unknown, isolated performer who must try to read the metaphor and recover the composer's meaning. That effort of interpretation forces the performer to step outside of the context of his own musical world into the context of the composer's as he tries to unravel the strands of metaphor and find the human being behind the printed notes. Though it might seem that the abstract, skeletal nature of printed music is fatally flawed because of its incompleteness—its inability to convey all of the rich nuances of musical speech—it is in fact this very incompleteness that is its greatest strength. This inability to completely convey a composer's intent creates participation and engagement on the part of performers, who will inevitably bring their own personalities into their search for the music's meaning. The fact that there can be so many different interpretations and performances of a piece of music is not a sign of its weakness but rather its strength.

When a piece of music is written down and sent off to others, it acquires a public life that is beyond any composer's control. It leaves the domain of "me" and enters the world of "we." And that can be a good thing, because in the best performances something gets created that neither the composer nor the performer could have envisioned by himself. Sigmund Freud said that we have no privileged position with respect to our own unconscious. Just because it is my mind, does not mean that I understand it completely or correctly. Analogously, just because it is the composer's piece, does not mean that only he knows how it should go. A composer's version of his own music (like a playwright's version of his own play) is also an interpretation. A well-known, Pulitzer prize–winning composer once told me that he felt fortunate to have had great performers teach him how his music should be played. The medium of printed music is inherently and blessedly incomplete. Notes are not final, nor should we wish them to be. They are the beginning of a dance with an unseen partner, who in the best cases understands and can see parts of the composer that the composer himself might never have known were there. A composer gets to write down the notes, but then he must let them go and turn them over into the hands of performers, who will bring the music to life in their own inexact, imperfect, subjective way. A piece of music's meaning is never fixed. It is perpetually changing, created in ongoing collaboration with unknown performers and listeners, one performance at a time.

GLOSSARY

arpeggio   From the Italian *arpeggiare*, meaning "to play the harp." Playing the notes of a chord one at a time instead of simultaneously.

augmentation   Playing a musical idea in lengthened note values, for example, playing it half or three times as slowly. (The opposite of diminution.)

Baroque period   The musical period lasting from approximately 1600 to 1750. Composers of this period include Georg Philipp Telemann, Johann Sebastian Bach, and Antonio Vivaldi. The term *baroque* comes from the Portuguese word *barroco*, meaning "an irregularly shaped pearl," which was originally a pejorative description of Italian painting and architecture in the 1600s.

bass line   The lowest voice in either an instrumental or vocal texture.

basso ostinato   Italian for "obstinate bass." The recurring bass line of a passacaglia. Also called a ground bass.

cadence   "A melodic or harmonic formula that occurs at the end of a section or phrase conveying the impression of a momentary or permanent conclusion." (*Harvard Dictionary of Music*)

canon   A piece of music in which multiple voices enter one after the other, singing or playing the identical melody. Like a round (e.g. "Row, Row, Row Your Boat").

chaconne   A series of continuous variations based on a recurring pattern of chords.

chord   Three or more notes played or sung at the same time.

Classical period   The musical period between the Baroque and Romantic eras extending roughly from 1750 to the early 1800s. Composers of this period include Josef Haydn, Wolfgang Amadeus Mozart, and Ludwig van Beethoven.

coda   A final concluding section of a piece of music that brings it to a convincing close.

codetta A short coda.

concerto A piece of music that features one or more soloists with orchestral accompaniment.

concerto grosso In Baroque music, a concerto featuring a small group of soloists, called the concertino, accompanied by a larger ensemble called the ripieno or concerto grosso, which gives the form its name.

counterpoint Music in which several independent melodic lines sound at the same time. The art of counterpoint lies in creating a texture where each individual line is satisfying and complete in and of itself yet also combines beautifully with the other parts.

crescendo Getting louder. A symbol telling the performer to increase volume. Sometimes abbreviated as *cresc.*

development In the sonata form, the second or middle section of a movement during which the materials of the exposition are developed.

diminished seventh chord A chord made of four notes, all a minor third (three half steps) apart. For example, B, D, F, A-flat.

diminution Playing a musical idea in shortened note values, for example, playing a musical idea twice or three times as fast. (The opposite of augmentation.)

dominant chord A major triad built on the fifth degree of a major or minor scale. In the key of C, the chord G, B, D. ("The" of "The End.")

dominant seventh chord A dominant chord with a seventh added. In the key of C, the chord G, B, D, F.

double exposition Refers to the form of a standard, first-movement, Classical-period concerto in which the main materials of the movement are introduced in two separate expositions: one for the orchestra alone that stays in the home key throughout, followed by a second exposition for soloist and orchestra that modulates.

exposition The first section of a movement in sonata form in which the materials of the piece are introduced or "exposed."

fermata A symbol telling the performer to hold a note or a rest longer than its written value. From the Italian *fermare*, meaning "to stop" or "to dwell on."

forte Italian for "loud."

fortissimo Italian for "very loud."

fugue A contrapuntal composition written for several musical parts or voices based on a main idea (called the subject) that is stated, then repeated and varied in continually changing contrapuntal combinations.

harmony The vertical or chordal structure of a piece of music. The particular chords formed by playing different notes simultaneously.

inversion (melodic) Changing a musical idea by turning it upside down so that each ascending interval becomes a descending interval and vice versa.

key The tonality of a particular composition, movement, or passage. A section or movement based on the C-minor scale is said to be in the key of C minor.

legato   Playing in such a way that notes are smoothly connected without audible breaks or separation.

measure   A basic unit of musical time, usually containing two, three, or four beats (though five or more are also possible), indicated by the time signature, and marked off in musical notation by bar lines.

melody   Tune. A group of notes played in succession that form a recognizable unit or phrase.

minuet   A formal courtly dance with three beats to the measure that was the predecessor to the waltz.

modulation   Changing keys within a section or movement. An important way to create harmonic variety in a piece.

motive or motif   A short, fragmentary musical idea often made up of only a few notes.

movement   A complete and fundamentally independent subdivision of a larger piece of music. For example, the first movement of a symphony or the slow movement of a concerto. Individual movements are usually (though not always) separated by pauses.

nocturne   A Romantic character piece, often written for the piano, that is usually meditative and melancholy in mood.

octave   An interval of seven half steps. The octave is the most perfect of all consonances with a frequency ratio of 2:1. Notes that are an octave apart (e.g., middle C on the piano and the C an octave higher) give the impression of being the same note.

passacaglia   A series of continuous variations over a repeating bass line.

pedal point   The term refers to a held or repeated note—usually in the bass—above which the upper parts change. Imagine an organist holding down a single note with a foot pedal throughout an entire passage.

period   The musical unit equivalent to a paragraph in written prose.

phrase   The musical unit equivalent to a sentence in written prose.

presto   Italian for "very fast."

recapitulation   The final section of a movement in sonata form in which the materials of the exposition return repeated, transposed to the home key, and resolved.

reharmonization   Repeating a melody or motive while changing the chords underneath.

ripieno   In Baroque orchestral music, the main orchestral group, as opposed to the solo group (the concertino).

ritornello   From the Italian meaning "little return." A passage that returns throughout a piece of music in literal or varied form. For example, the opening orchestral section of a Baroque concerto, or an instrumental interlude between the verses of a song or aria.

Romantic period   The musical era following the Classical period and extending approximately from 1820 to 1910. Composers in this period include Franz Schubert, Johannes Brahms, and Gustav Mahler.

rondo   A musical form frequently used as the final movement in Classical-period sonatas, concertos, and symphonies in which the opening melody returns several times (always in the home key) in alternation with contrasting music called episodes. If A is the rondo theme, with B and C representing contrasting music, the two most common rondo forms are ABACA or ABACABA.

scale   A succession of notes arranged in a particular fixed ascending and descending order. For example, a major scale, minor scale, or whole-tone scale.

scherzo   Italian for "joke." A quick, energetic movement, usually the third, which replaced the minuet in Classical-period sonatas, symphonies, and quartets. Like the minuet, the scherzo was also followed by a middle section called the trio and then a repeat of the scherzo. This basic scherzo-trio-scherzo format was expanded by Beethoven to scherzo-trio-scherzo-trio-scherzo.

sonata   An independent composition for a solo instrument or instruments usually made up of several movements.

sonata form   A term used to describe the form of individual movements of Classical- and Romantic-period sonatas, symphonies, quartets, and overtures. It is also referred to as sonata-allegro form or first-movement form because it is frequently used as the form for the first movement of a sonata.

stretto   In a fugue, the overlapping of entries of the theme. Like a round on the subject of a fugue.

syncopation   Shifting the normal accent in a measure or group of measures from a strong beat to a weak beat or to a position between beats.

theme   A musical idea that is the point of departure or subject of a composition.

tonic   The home note of a given key. In the key of C major, the note C is the tonic note.

tonic chord   The chord built on the home note of a given key. In the key of C major, a C-major chord is the tonic chord.

tutti   Italian for "all." In orchestral music, an indication that a passage is to be played by the whole orchestra as opposed to the soloists. In Baroque concertos a designation for sections in which the soloist(s) play(s) in unison with the full ensemble.

waltz   The most popular ballroom dance of the nineteenth century. A graceful, flowing, energetic dance in triple time—three beats to a measure.

CREDITS

Examples 3, 11, and 50: "I Got Rhythm," Music and Lyrics by George Gershwin and Ira Gershwin © 1930 (Renewed) WB Music Corp. All Rights Reserved. Gershwin® and George Gershwin® are registered trademarks of Gershwin Enterprises. Used by Permission of Alfred Publishing Co., Inc.

Examples 19 and 37: Leoš Janáček, Streichquartett, no. 2, *Intimate Letters* (Vienna: Philharmonia Partituren, 1928). Reprinted by permission.

Example 22: *The Soldier's Tale* by Igor Stravinsky. Libretto by Charles Ferdinand Ramuz. Copyright © 1924, 1987, 1992 for all countries Chester Music Ltd., 14-15 Berners Street, London W1T 3LJ, United Kingdom. All rights reserved. Reprinted by permission.

Example 26: "Piano Concerto in G Major" by Maurice Ravel © 1932 Ed. Durand S.A. (SACEM). Copyright renewed. All rights administered in the US and Canada by Universal Music–MGB Songs (ASCAP). Used by permission. All rights reserved.

Example 28: *Peter and the Wolf* by Sergei Prokofiev. Copyright © 1937 (Renewed) by G. Schirmer, Inc. (ASCAP) International copyright secured. All rights reserved. Reprinted by permission.

Example 30: *Requiem Canticles* by Igor Stravinsky. Copyright © 1967 by Boosey & Hawkes Music Publishers Ltd. Reprinted by permission.

Example 51: "Cheek to Cheek" from the RKO Motion Picture *Top Hat*. Words and Music by Irving Berlin © Copyright 1935 by Irving Berlin.

INDEX

NOTE: Page references in *italics* refer to musical compositions or illustrations.